MAGICKAL PLACES

MAGICKAL PLACES

A WICCAN'S GUIDE TO SACRED SITES AND SPIRITUAL CENTERS

Patricia Telesco

CITADEL PRESS
Kensington Publishing Corp.
www.kensingtonbooks.com

CONTENTS

ACKNOWLEDGMENTS

First, I gratefully and humbly acknowledge Mr. Martin Gray, P.O. Box 4111, Sedona, AZ (www.sacredsites.com), whose studies of sacred sites and efforts to preserve them are truly inspirational. Mr. Gray was extremely generous in giving me some superb research suggestions for which I cannot adequately thank him.

Thanks also go to the following individuals who took the time to write me about their experiences at different sites discussed in this book:

Blythe: Keith Bridge Park, Georgia; Bath, England
Laura Waters: Algiers Landing, Louisiana
Dave Ledwin: Valley of the Monuments, Arizona; Thunder Bay, Ontario; Brushwood, New York
Katherine Rickett: New Grange, Ireland
Shadow: Tallulah Gorge, Georgia
Sunny: various sites in Hawaii
Ofelas: Petroglyph National Monument, Arizona
Arawn: Arroyo Hondo, New Mexico (side trip for Rio Grande Gorge); Lookout Mtn., Tennessee; Benevento, Italy (side trip for Blue Grotto)
Ikyoto: various sites in Arizona, New Mexico, Texas, and Scotland

INTRODUCTION

Sacred places thus forge and strengthen bonds
between us and the universe in which we believe.
They empower us by affirming the wholeness
of the universe . . .
—THOMAS BENDER, *The Power of Place*

Throughout humankind's history we find people around the
world regarding nature with admiration, awe, and wonder.
When tribal societies developed animistic belief systems, for
example, the first things shaman-priests designated as having
sacred spirits were the land, its inhabitants, and the elements
within which humankind lived. As time wore on, this kind of
respect continued, experiencing minor philosophical changes
that suited our collective evolution. No matter the culture or setting, however, one communal belief echoed across the ages —
that the Creator's truths are revealed throughout creation and
especially by the earth.

Our ancestors believed that all the secrets of the universe
were somehow hidden in nature's storehouse, just waiting for discovery. So, over time, people categorized everything on the planet
according to its symbolic cosmic power. Each plant and animal

was given astrological, metaphysical, and/or elemental associations. These associations were then applied through religious and material procedures in the hopes of enhancing the quality of life, and slowly unraveling at least some of its mysteries.

While our scientific and technological knowledge has outgrown many superstitions and rituals, and we have forgotten many correspondences, Wiccans feel that the need to understand the earth's lessons and Her special form of magic has not waned. As an earth-centered religion, Wicca advocates returning to a lifestyle where spirituality walks hand in hand with real life—where we honor our home, the earth, as holy. By combining this philosophy and proactive global efforts, Wiccans are working toward re-establishing an earth-first awareness in the collective human soul. This book represents one such effort.

People desperately need an effective tool for reconnecting with the earth's spirit, the Great Spirit, and other sacred energies. With the busy nature of our world, these energies are often literally plowed under in the name of progress. Such devastation often cheats humanity out of a valuable opportunity: the chance to inspire our spiritual nature by getting to know our earthly parent more intimately, in all its beauty and power.

In an effort to forestall this destructive trend, *Magickal Places* revisits the precepts of sacred geometry and ecospirituality. These two philosophies challenge us to recognize and treat the earth as a temple. Using these ideologies and Wiccan beliefs as a foundation, this book furnishes information, guidance, and exercises aimed at improving your ability to recognize, interpret, harmonize with, integrate, and apply the earth's sacred energies for personal and planetary transformation. Within these pages, you'll find a cohesive system for a spiritual renaissance using the earth's sacred sites and power centers as a starting point.

While many of these places bear familiar names, not all such sites are renowned or well known. Indeed, to an unwary passerby, some might appear as nothing more than a grove of trees or pile of rubble. But appearances can be deceiving. Lessons and beauties surround us every day, in things as simple as a pebble and as sublime as the stars. Even a nearby patch of grass houses tremendous magical potential. All it takes is looking at it with an appreciative, expectant eye. That dandelion, for example, may be a pesty weed to some, but for Wiccans it represents divinatory ability, wish magic, and the goddess Hecate!

With this amazing potential in mind, *Magickal Places* takes you on a global adventure to rediscover the power of the earth's ley lines, vortexes, megaliths, and magic. It begins with insights and cues that will help you recognize sacred spaces, their elemental associations, and their potential to manifest positive personal or global changes. The guide then discusses creating power spots yourself that will be filled with your own vision and magic. Note that these energy centers need not be created in the wilderness—you can make them nearly anywhere, anytime! In fact, considering our need for more positive energy in the city, creating sacred sites in apartments, garages, and on street corners may be exactly what urbania needs to begin healing!

Last, but not least, you will visit some of the world's most beautiful spiritual centers via the written word. Each of these listings includes history, local lore, travel considerations, and elemental correspondences. Each also includes step-by-step activities to augment and manifest that region's energies in your reality in life-affirming ways.

Magickal Places offers a hands-on chance to improve your perception of nature's power and internalize that awareness. It stresses the need to be continually aware of, and responsive to, the sacred space represented by the earth and every corner of it. This undertaking doesn't offer "quick fixes," but with time and tenacity it does offer concrete results in both the spiritual and material worlds.

If we start to live sensitively, reverently, and in reciprocity with nature, this cannot help but change us in astounding ways. The natural outcome of aware, responsive living in the long haul is nothing short of global transformation. We will begin to see how the Sacred Parent exists in every blade of grass and every flower, and, perhaps most important, within each of us. Second, we will begin to act and live differently—honoring our planet and one another—because of this new perspective. Considering some of the serious global issues facing the human race, this seems to be a sensible step in the right direction.

So, travel with me now to the sacred sites established by both our ancestors and some of our modern-day visionary companions. At each site described herein, you'll discover radiant divine power and the planet's shining spirit. Once experienced and understood, these two lights will illuminate your soul and guide the way to a better future for both the earth and you.

Part I

THE LEY
OF THE LAND

> **In belonging to a landscape, one feels a rightness,
> at-homeness, a knitting of self and world.**
> —SCOTT RUSSELL SANDERS, *Staying Put*

It is truly sacred ground on which we walk. Nothing that lives in, on, or above the earth is corrupt or "evil" in its pure form. It is, instead, dormant and neutral. The concept of goodness or badness doesn't occur until we actively do something to create or activate positive or negative energy. So the outcome of our exploration and use of sacred sites, both metaphysically and substantively, depends totally on how we humans decide to use this gift called earth.

This chapter therefore examines the earth's gift to us as a living organism filled with magical potential. Why? Because it's hard to be interested in preserving something if you don't understand what could be lost. Because it's nearly impossible to work with an energy source if you don't know how to recognize and direct it. And because, as spiritual seekers, it's vital that we reconnect with our Earth Mother to nurture our souls into wholeness.

Where does the earth's spiritual sustenance originate? In life itself. All life creates energy. Science tells us that this energy cannot be destroyed; it only changes shape. This means the earth and its inhabitants (plants and animals alike) generate vast amounts of power each day—power that you can use for personal or planetary transformation.

Ah, but don't go jumping into your ritual robe just yet. Think of spells and rituals as one strand in life's network. When you work magic, energy goes out along that strand to manifest your goal. But if you don't have a good feel for the bends and intersections that the spell or ritual may encounter, you'll likely find your magical efforts tied up in knots! So before you grasp the earth's fibers of force and weave them into positive magic, you have to first recognize the basic patterns that indicate power and the patterns created out of that power.

Chapter 1

THE EARTH'S AURA

That one vast thought of God which we call the world.
— BULWER LYTTON

Wiccans feel that executing a positive magical path depends in part on (1) getting to know our home on a different level than normal awareness allows, and (2) acting on that knowledge, both physically and spiritually. The first step to achieving goal number one is to realize that Wiccans do not view the earth as simply a nondescript body of stone and soil. It has a spirit that needs to be considered in our magical equation. Just as the human spirit shapes and colors our body's auric envelope (recognizable in body heat), the earth's spirit shapes and colors the planetary aura. Think of this as a spiritual atmosphere that touches all things and extends out into space.

This means that when we seek to achieve goal number two by working with earth energies, our magic extends much further than one might initially think! It also means that when earth's aura is damaged or out of balance, it has far-reaching effects that we're only beginning to comprehend. On a mundane level, for example, the pollution in the atmosphere makes people, plants, and animals sick. It leaches into the soil through rain, and thereby continues a cycle of dis-ease instead of wellness.

Similarly, when a region of land is injured through war or construction, everything around that area is affected along with everything that exists along any connecting energy lines (today called ley lines). For example, animals might leave the area. The soil might be damaged and unusable for agriculture, and thus neighboring ecosystems are intruded upon (including the human ones). If you extend this intrusion along life's weblike network, you can quickly see how even small problems can have extensive repercussions.

On a spiritual level, injuries to the earth disrupt the earth's aura because it's composed of this planet's vital energy. Effectively, pollution, overpopulation, and other human intrusions into the ecosystem make earth's aura sick. Everything within that aura is then subject to the same dis-ease. The outward manifestations of this in our society include corruption, war, transience, and apathy. The inward impact can only be gauged by each individual doing a little soul searching.

One way to correct some of the harm done is by preserving, augmenting, repairing, and working with the earth's known power centers (Stonehenge is one example), and by creating more like them everywhere possible (see later in this chapter). In such regions, sacred energies radiate outward, networking each-to-each, holding us and the planet in loving, regenerative arms. By applying these powers and using magic to guide them, we can begin the process of global, societal, and personal auric rejuvenation.

It's Element-ary

An elemental force is ruthlessly frank.
— Joseph Conrad

The earth's aura is comprised of energy from the elements—the basic building blocks of all life. Wiccans wholeheartedly believe that these elements hold important clues to understanding the

greater mysteries. In addition, with Wicca and several other esoteric traditions, each element (earth-air-fire-water-spirit/ether)
has a specific habitat, inhabitants, intelligence, and powers all its
own. A basic understanding of these elemental correspondences
is important to discovering, working with, and/or creating
sacred sites.

Think of an element like a note of music. Not all notes
vibrate harmoniously with all other notes. As you seek out and
approach a sacred site, or consider creating one, knowing its
keynote helps you tap that energy sensitively and intuitively. Just
as you wouldn't randomly begin singing during an opera perfor-
mance, it's unseemly to interrupt, change, or redirect the music of
a site without appreciating it and knowing what you're doing.

So, the following section reviews the elements briefly, along
with their correspondences. Consider this information when
you're looking for a specific type of energy center for a spell or
ritual. For example, if you're seeking an appropriate region for
a healing ritual or spell, you might go to a sacred site with a
predominant water element. Similarly, when you're creating
sacred spaces yourself, you may want to align them with one or
more specific elements to augment whatever type of magic you
plan to perform there.

As you read, please realize that the names of the elements
and their designations often experience cultural variations. So,
I'm limiting this particular exploration to the most common associations in Wiccan practice. Consequently, the elemental associations of some sacred places will change according to the traditions
that created them, the cultures in which they reside, and the like.
This is where you'll have to let your intuition guide you.

Also, as you seek out, enjoy, or make sacred sites, bear in
mind that the elements don't exist in a vacuum. Most areas
exhibit secondary elements that can further your "element-ary"
education and augment your magic.

Earth

The earth element is sometimes hard to define in a sacred site, because so many have strong earthly energies. Sites located on farms, plains, valleys, and underground structures like caves often have a predominant earth element. Any area that makes you feel really grounded, rooted, focused, stable, nurtured, healthy, peaceful, safe, and/or methodical is likely an earth-energy center. These sensations are also the characteristics of earth-energies as applied in magic (and at the sites given herein). For example, a person might sit on the soil after a spell to ground out energy, or plant a seed in rich loam so magic can grow.

Another way to recognize an earth center is by its spiritual voice. Earth centers have a profound heartbeat, akin to a drum, that reverberates like an echo in a deep cave. To hear this sound, place your ear to the soil, quiet yourself, and just listen. Be patient; it takes time to develop this skill.

According to tradition, the beings that frequent earth sites are the elves, brownies, gnomes, and dwarves, all of whom live close to the land. These creatures are tenacious, helpful, and hard working, so they dislike lazy humans. On the other hand, when you need a little extra money or seek to improve your ability to work with the land, these beings can prove quite helpful. If you're not familiar with working with elementals, I suggest you read my book *Dancing with Devas: Elemental Magic* (Toad Hall Press, 1998).

In the magical circle, the earth element is placed at the northern point and is associated with the season of winter, the sense of touch, and the hour of midnight. This information might be useful when performing special activities at earth sites. For example, place your hands on the rocks, plants, or soil when communing with the energy there, to "feel" the power. Or, hold a ritual at one of these sites at midnight to honor that power.

Air

The air element is the most elusive to pin down because it touches all things. Sites located on cliffs, peaks, towers, and other high, windy grounds, often have a predominant air element. Any area that makes you feel playful, inspired, stimulated, contemplative, independent, and communicative is likely an air-energy center. These sensations are the characteristics of air-energies as applied in magic (and at the sites given herein). For example, people might cast flower petals to a wind blowing toward them in a spell for creativity.

Another way to recognize an air center is by its music. Air centers have a voice like the earth, but it is lighter, often sound-

ing like chimes or bells. To hear this sound, stand in a breeze, quiet yourself, and just listen. Note that different winds have drastically different songs. A full gale sounds of large, violently ringing bells, whereas a summer zephyr tinkles with joy.

According to tradition, the beings that frequent air sites are the sylphs, who are airy, etherial, and breathtakingly lovely. Folkloric accounts claim that the sylphs carry oracular messages from the gods to human ears. In personality traits, these creatures embody capriciousness, open mindedness, and zeal. When you need a little motivation or to improve your psychic ability, these powers can prove quite helpful.

In the magical circle, the air element is placed at the eastern point and is associated with the season of spring, the sense of smell, the hour of dawn, and the emotion of hopefulness. This information might be useful when performing special activities at air sites. For example, reach your hands out toward a fresh wind at dawn and welcome renewed hope into your heart. Or include a breath-centered meditation at the site as a way of better attuning yourself to this element and the region's power.

Fire

The fire element is the most temperamental and the hardest to control because of its intensity. Sites located in the desert, in arid regions, at volcanos, near hot springs, or those with a central hearth/fire source often have a predominant fire element. Any area that makes you feel empowered, passionate, purified, inventive, loving, or righteous is likely a fire-energy center. These sensations are the characteristics of fire-energies as applied in magic (and at the sites given herein). For example, a person might place a picture of someone before a candle flame to illuminate hidden matters in that relationship.

Another way to recognize a fire center is by its noises. Fire centers have a boisterous crackle about them. To hear this sound, sit before a fire source, quiet yourself, and just listen. Note that small fires have a slower, more tempered sound, whereas a bonfire will reverberate with exuberance.

According to tradition, the beings that frequent fire sites are the salamanders, who appear like a single tongue of flame. Folkloric accounts claim that these creatures embody fervor, enthusiasm, joy, excitement, sexual energy, and spiritual power. When you need to renew the warmth in a relationship or shine a light on the shadows in your life, these powers can prove quite helpful.

In the magical circle, the fire element is placed at the southern point and is associated with the season of summer, the sense of sight, the hour of noon, and affectionate emotions. This information might be useful when performing special activities at fire sites. For example, go to the site at noon, turn yourself so you're facing south, then cast a spell for improved physical energy. Or, include a visualization of light filling you from the site as a way of banishing negative thought patterns or bad habits.

Water

The water element is the most gentle in some ways and yet very strong (note that with time water wears away the greatest of

rocks). Sites located in misty areas, in the rainforest, on lake shores, on river banks, adjacent to waterfalls or geysers, or near fountains often have a predominant water element. Any area that makes you feel insightful, healthy, cleansed, patient, maternal, or fertile is likely a water-energy center. These sensations are the characteristics of water-energies as applied in magic (and at the sites given herein). For example, a person might drink a cup of magically charged spring water as part of a spell for health.

Another way to recognize a water center is by its vibrational wave. Water centers have a sound that is difficult to describe; it's like a mix of rain falling lightly on grass and a wave crashing to shore. To hear this, just pick up an old seashell and put it to your ear! Note that, as with the other elements, different types of water have different sounds. Just compare a waterspout or monsoon to a spring downpour.

According to tradition, the beings that frequent water sites are the undines who appear much like the merpeople of myths and legends. Folkloric accounts claim that these creatures embody versatility, love, intuition, and pure beauty. When you need to smooth over a situation or heal a broken heart, these powers can prove quite helpful.

In the magical circle, the water element is placed at the western point and is associated with the season of autumn, the sense of taste, the hour of twilight, and instinctive feelings. This information might be useful when performing special activities at water sites. For example, go to the site at dusk with a cup of water, and pour it out as a way of welcoming the undines and asking for their aid. Or, visualize yourself being filled with spiritual water to improve personal empathy.

Spirit

The spirit element represents the bond between the other four and is the essence of magic. Sites that seem to blend all elements together, those located in the center of circular patterns or labyrinths, or those that have mirror images often have a predominant spirit element. Any area that makes you feel limitless, eternal, all-connected, karmically aware, and coherent is likely a spirit-energy center. These sensations are the characteristics of spirit-energies as applied in magic (and at the sites given herein). For example, Wiccans work within a magic circle to raise and direct magic.

Another way to recognize a spirit center is by its subtle blending of all elemental sounds. Spirit is infamously quiet, but very distinct to each person in a personal way. To hear this, listen to the sounds of your breath and your heart beating, then keep listening. Eventually, you will discover the still, small voice of spirit within your own soul.

In the magical circle, the spirit element is placed at the center point and is associated with the ever-turning Wheel of the Year, the sense of hearing, the hour of eclipses, and spiritual or devout emotions. This information might be useful when performing special activities at spirit sites. For example, go to the site at night and look upon the stars and galaxies, then visualize them as part of your own heart. Or, go to the site during the night of a lunar or solar eclipse and listen closely to see what messages spirit may have for you.

Chapter 2

SACRED SITES

Now that we know the key components that exist within nature and form the matrix within which all life hums, the next question seems obvious. What's the difference between a plain old rock that represents earth and a rock that's part of an earth power center?

Throughout the ages, artists, seers, philosophers, priests, and sages alike tried to answer this question for us by using their talents. These people and others like them applied spiritual insights to design, adorn, and/or honor various places around the globe that, to this day, arouse awe and admiration. From the Taj Mahal to the petroglyphs of New Mexico, Wiccans believe that the locations and designs chosen for each site were not random or happenstance.

From a magical perspective, we believe the ancients were devising a kind of signpost for others to follow, indicating the patterns of earth's power. Some of these patterns seem to spiral, indicating a vortex. Other patterns were lines: what Victorians might have called fairy paths or what we call ley lines. The third most predominant pattern was the sacred circle, revealing a power center or area in which ley lines intersect.

Today, these signposts become a spiritual blueprint that we can follow in recognizing what constitutes a sacred place, how to work with that place, and even how to make our own sacred places. From a temporal perspective, each location has a unique story to tell that's influenced by numerous environmental, historical, and cultural factors. From a spiritual perspective, however, one underlying truth exists. The cornerstone to every sacred site, both past and present, near and far, is a nucleus of spiritual energy—an electricity in the air and land that's unmistakable.

A sacred site has unbridled power of various degrees coursing through it. This energy might be generated by a nature deva. It might have been inspired by a momentous event, a cultural myth, a religious fable, or from ongoing use for spiritual purposes by any number of people. In other cases, the energy is natural outflowing of the earth's heartbeat or a direct line to and from the Sacred Powers. Whatever the reason, this river of life-energy exists on a higher plane of awareness, something to which Wiccans try to remain open and aware.

With that said, what was built upon this spiritual cornerstone—how people directed and augmented that base energy—depended much on the vision of the unsuspecting wanderer who happened to discover its power, be that person a peasant, prophet, or pope! So how do we go about interpreting personal or religious vision? What exactly were these people trying to communicate to future generations by etching Celtic knotwork on a vortex's headstone, building an archway over a power center, or writing about the voice of God in creation? Were they simply drawing our attention to that spot, or was there more to it?

Perhaps part of the key to understanding comes through a message left behind by past shamans, monks, and village wisepeople alike: that we are but stewards of the earth, not its owners. Wiccans and all spiritual seekers should be trying to guide and use earth-energies for the greatest good. We should continue the legacy of honoring, caretaking, augmenting, and worshiping at these beautiful places so future generations can benefit from their powers, too—a duty that has been sorely neglected until recently.

THE REBIRTH OF ECOSPIRITUALITY

Nature is an Aeolian harp, a musical instrument, whose tones are the re-echo of higher strings within us.

—NOVALIS

The environmental crisis has brought religious leaders from all walks of life into the political arena seeking aid. In 1987 Pope John Paul stated that while humans dominate the earth, this didn't constitute the authority to abuse what god has given. In his statement the pope mirrored what ecospirituality has been saying for hundreds of years: that we are in partnership with the planet, and that this partnership has become very lopsided. To balance out the equation, ecospirituality advocates a hands-on, practical approach to reconciling our relationship with the earth, each other, and ourselves. This approach combines concrete efforts, personal vision, a heightened awareness of nature, and spiritual energy (or for Wiccans, magic).

In the ecospirituality model, the human body is a very real part of the planetary body. If we ever question this truth, one need only look to how many natural things can cure or kill us. Mirroring this connectedness is the Wiccan rede of "as within, so without." In other words, we cannot hope to find wholeness ourselves without healing the planet, too. As any good physician knows, it's very hard to treat a patient when you don't *know* that person. Taking this one step further, if we don't know creation, how can we expect to build a vital relationship with the Creator?

So where does one begin? First, accept the Sacred as part of all things, including yourself. Every stone, brook, leaf, insect, animal, and twig has a story to tell and a lesson to share. We just have to slow down long enough to listen. Second, honor this sacredness in the way you live, the way you think, and the way you treat the world.

Third, remember that Wicca prescribes a way of be-ing present and attentive each day—a lifestyle that is earth-centered and earth-friendly whenever possible. Approach each morning, each moment of living, as an opportunity to learn and grow as a spiritual being. Approach the earth as the classroom for this learning process, the spirits of nature and sacred places as teachers, and the Sacred Parent as the principal and founder of your quest.

WHY VISIT MAGICKAL PLACES?

Don't wait to be ready. Everything you need for this journey is available to you right now.
—K. BRADFORD BROWN

One way to reintegrate the ecospirituality model into our lives and reconnect with the Sacred Parent is by using nature as a letter of introduction, natural laws as our prototype, and the earth's sacred sites as stimulation. We would certainly not be the first people to try this approach! In fact, many of the earth's religious traditions advocate pilgrimages to a particular site or sites as part of a religious life's learning process.

Why? Because a small spark of the divine exists in each atom of creation, holding everything together and guiding life's music like a great conductor might. Whether you experience this ancient song when tending your windowbox garden, sitting beneath an old tree, or visiting a known sacred site, one cannot help but be fundamentally moved and changed by the experience. In these truly magical moments you, the earth, and the heavens waltz together to the music of the spheres. At that instant there need be no separation between you and the sky, you and an animal, you and others, you and the world. All are one; all are special; all are sacred; all are divine.

FINDING SACRED SITES

True holiness comes wrapped in the ordinary.
—MACRINA WIEDERKEHR, *A Tree Full of Angels*

As spiritual seekers, Wiccans hope to use elemental and earth-energies respectfully and for the greatest good. Even so, we recognize that religious conviction and everyday reality don't always work cooperatively. For example, not all of us can travel the world over just to experience the earth's famous power centers. Thankfully, it's not as difficult as you might think to find a sacred site nearby. Places you hid as a child, places that you retreat to in times of stress, and others like them have a special ambiance that draws you in—a holiness, a womb of energy. These are power centers and sacred as long as you treat them accordingly.

When I was young, I always found myself singing to a grouping of trees and a raspberry bush near a creek when life became difficult. The trees never minded if I was off key, the bush supplied snacks, and the creek seemed to sing along. When that area was plowed under to make room for an apartment complex, I cried for a week. It was indeed a sanctuary and I still miss it, especially now that I understand what was lost.

So think about where you live. Are there any waterfalls, caves, groves, odd stone outcroppings, neat parks, and so forth, in close proximity? Have you driven by or been to an area that somehow felt "special"? If you're new to your region or can't think of any places that have really "called" to you, get out and walk your neighborhood and other nearby bits of land . . . a small children's park will do for starters. Sometimes all we need do is give nature an opportunity to speak.

As you walk, open all your senses. Watch for trees, stones, or plants that form patterns like circles. Look for brightly colored grasses that streak through a field of darker grass (called fairy paths). These often follow ley lines and in folklore are believed to be trodden by the fey themselves. Listen for the enchanting call of a bird, feel a vibrantly alive wind, smell a uniquely scented flower—let the citizens of nature guide you to a sacred place all your own.

Other strong indicators of a power center or sacred site include:

- A powerful energy current that makes you tingle all the while you're there
- A presence that makes you feel in good company, peaceful, and welcome
- A strong physical or emotional reaction to a region that you can't wholly quantify
- A feeling that time has stopped and nothing exists but this moment, this place, you, and the sacred
- An awareness that nature or its citizens are trying to provide you with omens or other messages whenever you visit a particular place
- A frequent visit by the earthly representative of your power animal(s) in one specific spot
- A place that bears a striking resemblance to a recent, spiritually centered dream (or a place that you regularly dream about after visiting it)
- A place that has unusually large, brightly colored, or healthy plant growth compared to the neighboring regions

Finding such regions may take a little time and patience, but I'm willing to bet you will become a better student of nature, signs, and dream imagery for the effort.

Note too that manmade objects and buildings can exhibit amazing sacredness if they were designed by someone sensitive. This means that you may discover a unique fountain, a piece of graffiti, a park statue, a historical home, or other buildings that evoke strong, unanticipated spiritual feelings. When this occurs, don't discount what you're experiencing just because it bears a human touch. Even as nature carries a divine imprint, so does the human soul—meaning an architect, artist, woodworker, and others can make a sacred site just by the love, talent, and insight he or she puts into the effort.

In addition, there is always the possibility that a structure may have been built on a ley line, vortex, or other type of energy center. A good example of this happens when someone finds his or her house haunted because it was built on the site of an old, forgotten cemetery. The cemetery constitutes holy ground, and when it was disturbed so were the residents! A more positive illustration might be a statue of the Virgin Mary that evokes strong connections to the Goddess because it's located on or near earth's heartbeat.

If you still can't seem to find any energy centers, or just aren't sure if you've found one, dousing offers another way to locate and confirm sacred sites, ley lines, and power spots. Think of a douser's rod like the needle in a compass, except that in the hands of a spiritually aware person, it's sensitive to a wider variety of magnetic and auric energies. There are different kinds of dousing rods available in New Age gift shops, but the most popular ones for finding ley lines and vortexes are made of two L-shaped metal bars.

To try using these yourself, hold the short end of the L in your grasp. The long part is parallel to the ground and straight out in front of you. Begin walking over an area, thinking of what you hope to find. When the two bars cross in the middle, it's called a "hit." Note your results secretively, and then have another person double-check the accuracy using the same method. Once the results are confirmed, create an energy map, marking that spot along with any other hits.

Finally, look for patterns like common geometric figures (lines, squares, circles, triangles, etc.). Circles are usually power spots or vortexes, while lines are usually ley lines. If any power points and ley lines cross over and/or surround an area, this spot has the greatest potential to house earth-energies.

By working in or near this region, you can augment and channel these energies into life-affirming magic. Just make sure your presence is allowed (e.g., don't trespass on posted land or a site considered off limits to all but practitioners of a particular faith). While it might be tempting to try and sneak in, respecting other people and their traditions indirectly shows respect for the spirits of a region. It also goes a long way toward building tolerance and understanding among people of different paths.

Once you do find a site you consider sacred and can visit regularly, honor it somehow. Bring spring water to the land, mark it with stones, or plant crystals in the soil. Dedicate the land, then cast spells, meditate, and perform rituals there. The more you extend magic to the spot, and the more you work with the earth-energies there, the more power will radiate from that area. This power becomes like a healing salve that spreads as far as the eye can see and beyond, blessing everything and everyone it touches, including *you*!

THE PERSONAL PILGRIMAGE

**The gods seemed to have possessed my soul and turned
it inside out, and roadside images seemed to invite me
from every corner, so that it was impossible for me to
stay at home.**

—BATSU BASHO

Once you find a sacred site that truly calls to your heart, and
you have the wherewithal to go there, you must understand that
the journey to a power center—be it here or across the globe—
is not simply a nifty vacation or side trip. In studying the paths
taken by pilgrims around the world to sacred sites, we discover
that this is an important spiritual undertaking that seems to have
certain stages associated with it. These stages are:

One: Preparation Here the individual takes time to
cleanse herself through ritual baths, fasting, abstinence, and
prayer so that she is pure and pleasing to the spirits of a place
and the divine.

Two: The First Step All great journeys begin this way,
with something to mark the transition from what was to what
can be. Sometimes this "thing" is an outward statement, like cut-
ting one's hair or accepting a taboo. In other cases it is simply an
inner change in attitude from mundane to esoteric.

Three: Release Here you acknowledge a partnership
between you and the powers with which you're working in
co-creating personal or planetary transformations. An old Gaelic
charm expresses this cooperation very well. It says: *god over me,
under me, before me, behind me. I on thy path o god, thou o god in my
steps.*

Four: Attentiveness and Awareness During this stage
you really refine your goals and purpose, and then begin honing

all your senses to achieving those aims and receiving whatever message the spirits have for you.

Five: Struggle, Persistence, Overcoming   For whatever reason a pilgrimage is rarely embarked on without some type of difficulties. The barriers test your spiritual mettle and determination. To what extent are you willing to keep trying to achieve your goals? How patient can you be? Was it worth all the trouble? These are the kinds of questions that arise in stage five, for which you must find adequate answers.

Six: Relearning and Reawakening   This is what I call the "Ah ha!" point, where the proverbial light bulb goes on, and everything comes together and finally fits. No matter what your initial intention was in coming to a sacred site, the *real* reason for you being here is illuminated in your mind and soul. Stage six often has life-changing ramifications and is typically very hard to verbalize to others because of its intimacy.

Seven: Reflection and Integration   Stage seven often happens during the journey home and is frequently accompanied by tears, laughter, and other emotional releases. Without reflection and integration your experience will fade into a distant memory, so let it happen, take notes, and meditate on your insights often. The more you do, the more this place and this experience will become an active part of daily reality.

Throughout the multi-stage process, the pilgrim is always aware that the journey may be physical but it affects far more than just the body. Traveling to a sacred site is as much an inward quest as it is outward and upward. So look within, extend your senses to the energies around you, and reach up to the heavens for your answers and aid.

Chapter 3

CREATING YOUR OWN
SACRED SPACE

**Wherever you live is your temple
if you treat it like one.**
— BUDDHA

When you can't find a sacred site, or travel to a known one, you need not feel at a loss. Early people were in a similar boat — they had few, if any, sacred places already established for them and were unable to travel far to seek them out. So, they got creative and made their own, many of which we still enjoy today and use as prototypes!

How did they achieve this? Our ancestors observed the patterns in nature when determining the placement and design for temples, burial sites, and other sacred structures. The final expression of these patterns depended much on the culture, era, and individual(s) in charge of the project. Some used the designs to decorate the walls of a structure, like those seen in labyrinths and burial chambers. Some people marked sacred land with megaliths and dolmans, like Stonehenge and New Grange. Still others made sacred spaces inside the earth, like the Oracle at Delphi, creating a womb to nurture energy.

Many sacred sites seem to be laid out in line (along ley lines) with one another, or in a configuration. Sacred geologists and other people in the modern metaphysical community have begun mapping this pattern, which ties the whole world together into an energy matrix. Because of construction, war, and other man-made intrusions into the natural world, many lines along the map are no longer whole. When an incomplete, disrupted, or destroyed pattern is perceived, these mystical naturalists try to repair the damage using earth-awareness and the energy map to guide the work. In effect, they create sacred sites to positively repair and channel the powers that humanity interrupted, and you can do likewise!

One excellent example of this is the reemerging art of Feng Shui, which originated in China. Feng Shui masters might be considered an odd combination of artist and scientist. They use their knowledge and awareness of the earth's spirit (*qi*) to determine where and how to build places of worship, burial sites, birth sites, and homes. If structures already exist, the Feng Shui master looks at the land's natural curves and energy, then adjusts the living space to augment the most positive powers.

This is the type of awareness and knowledge you'll want to hone in creating your own sacred spaces. It's not necessarily something that can be "taught"—a better description is that you "feel" rightness deep within. In this section I have given you an overview of how to create several indoor and outdoor sacred sites and power centers, both large and small, but this is a guideline at best. Let your senses, your inner voice, guide each effort.

And don't let personal feelings of artistic inadequacy hold you back. Unlike the modern notion that fancy means better, in nature, and often in magic, simplicity has tremendous power and beauty. Holiness is something you create with your actions and attitude, not necessarily through trappings. Even some of the smallest efforts to create a special feeling—moving a stone,

burning aromatics, planting a flower, or changing decorations—
can have potent, transformational results.

THE HOME ALTAR

**Holiness is religious principle put into action—it is
faith gone to work—it is love coined into conduct.**
—F. D. HUNTINGTON

Your home is the most influential sacred space in your life. This
is where you, and those you love, make each day. From this
source—this spot of beginning and ending, primping and relax-
ing—existence takes shape. Consequently, the home altar should
not only reflect your personal beliefs, needs, and tastes, but
should also signify the importance of spiritual pursuits in your
everyday life.

By definition, an altar is a "high place"—a meeting ground
where earth and heaven, you and the divine, commune. Since
the goal of modern magical living is to become one with the
god/dess within us and around us, in some respects you can
think of your entire living space as an altar—a surface upon
which you can design visions of your path and the divine. Art,
candles, crystals, aromatics, and even certain kinds of furniture
offer numerous options for magical decorating schemes. This, in
and of itself, won't necessarily create sacred space, but it's a
good starting point. When you're done, every corner of your
home will be ready to absorb whatever magical energy you provide, then will disengage it slowly like a time-released spiritual
vitamin!

In a more traditional sense, a home altar is usually a table,
mantle, entertainment center top, kitchen counter, or other flat
surface upon which personally significant religious tools abide.

The layout of these objects, and exactly what's included, varies according to tradition and personal whimsy. Among Wiccans, the tools often get placed atop a special cloth in suitable elemental quarters around a central god or goddess image, for example:

- Western Quarter: bowl of water, cup, seashell, fountain, blue items, nori (seaweed), driftwood wands, images of sea creatures
- Northern Quarter: soil, plain stone, seeds, brown or dark green items, wooden wand, potted plants, images of land-dwelling creatures, favored pets, or plants
- Eastern Quarter: feather, bells, a fan, yellow or white items, images of birds, smudge stick, natural items heavily influenced by the winds (like leaves)
- Southern Quarter: burning candle, incense, brazier, red or orange items, athame (ritual dagger), images of desert-dwelling creatures
- God/dess images: statuary, framed picture, candle, round stones (goddess), oblong stones (god)

For those of you reading this who have little space for such elaborate set-ups, there is a nice alternative. Find a hollow sphere that can be divided into two halves. Fill one half with elemental tokens that have strong personal meaning for you. Close the sphere using a strong adhesive and decorate the edge with ribbon that has a loop for hanging. You now have a functional "knickknack" that will fit almost anywhere (including your car) to become a completely portable altar.

Once you've chosen what type of altar you want, where you want to put it (safely out of reach of children and pets), and what items it will house, the next step is cleansing. Basically, you want to ensure that the tokens you place on the altar are

purified of unwanted energies. Magic works best when trans-
mitted through a clean channel. If you think of how many
people handled those items before you, and the residual feelings
they may have left behind, it's easy to understand the importance of this step. Purification can be accomplished by soaking
the items in salt water, passing them through the smoke of
cleansing incense (sage, cedar, or pine are good choices), or by
visualizing each being filled to overflowing with white, sparkling
light. The choice of approach is purely personal.

Next, you want to consecrate the altar for its intended func-
tion. Hold your hands palms down over the surface and pray
(or chant) in any manner suited to your beliefs. Light a candle
for a few minutes to represent the presence of the divine. Then,
invite the Powers of Creation to bless the area and saturate it
with sacredness. If you have a specific god or goddess whom
you follow, now would be a good time to invoke his or her presence. This altar, after all, will be the symbolic seat of that
god/dess where you welcome him or her into your sacred space
of home during worship.

Your altar is a potent nucleus for your faith — holy and magical — augmenting whatever energy you create from that day forward. Once consecrated, this surface becomes a central location
for prayer, spells, rituals, and spiritual studies. Say good morning to the Universal Powers here each day. Meditate nearby.
Make or bless charms on the altar's surface. Leave offerings for
your god/dess here in thankfulness when your magic manifests.
Or, just sit near the altar for improved understanding when
you're reading a favorite magical text.

Like any mystical region, the more an altar gets used, the
more of your personal vibrations mingle with that of the god/dess,
further empowering the site. This energy then radiates throughout
your living space, and beyond. More important, in those moments
when your schedule leaves little time for focusing on the sacred,

a home altar keeps your spiritual path active and vital simply by continuing to radiate the magic you've placed there.

THE ELEMENTAL LIVING SPACE

A place will express itself through the human being just as it does through the wild flowers.
—LAWRENCE DURRELL

Going back to the earlier discussion regarding the elements and the creatures that abide therein, another way of creating sacred space within your home is by accenting the directional correspondences using well-considered, charged decorations. Really, these can be anything: a crystal, some silk flowers, a painting, a specific pattern on a mouse pad, a lamp with a colored light bulb, or other knickknacks. What's important is that the chosen object mirrors the elemental quarter that it will reside in, and that it's meaningful to you.

The extra benefit in using an elemental decorating scheme is that it's very subtle. People who don't know what they're looking at (specifically, those who might be skittish about Wicca) will think you're just very creative with home embellishments! Here are some examples of ways to accent a single room or your entire house:

- Eastern Quarter: Pale yellow items; an open window blind (to let the morning sun in); wind chimes; a fan or air conditioner; artistic renderings of birds or fairies; a feather duster.
- Southern Quarter: Red or orange items; decorative candles; a lamp; sun catchers; a stove, microwave, toaster oven, or area heater; artistic renderings of deserts or desert creatures; a cactus.

- Western Quarter: Blue or purple items; a decorative cup or bowl; a faucet, water cooler, or indoor fountain; seashells, driftwood, or sand art; artistic renderings of the ocean, beach, or animals that dwell in those areas.
- Northern Quarter: Brown or dark green items; a potted plant; pottery; natural crystal bookends; indoor rock garden; decorative seed or grain bottles; artistic renderings of farmland, plains, trees, or indigenous animals.

Some living spaces don't allow for exact placement of symbolic objects, so don't worry if your water symbol doesn't rest directly due west. Be more concerned with the overall effect — the way the object and its location changes the ambiance of your living space. If it feels right and leaves you with a sense of peace and belonging, then you've done a great job!

To charge your chosen tokens for their purpose, you can pray over them, meditate with them, place them in sunlight or moonlight (whichever seems more suited to the token and its magical purpose; sunlight accents the conscious/masculine self, while moonlight augments the intuitive/feminine nature), or visualize them being filled with light energy. Before placing each into the appropriate spot in your home, decide on words that will activate the tokens energy any time you feel the need, and other words to deactivate it. (For example, you might actually use the words "magic on" and "magic off" as your activating phrases.) Whisper these words into the token three times, noting which is which, then put the object where you wish.

This approach successfully accomplishes three things. First, it creates an informal sacred space around your home that's in place at all times to protect and nurture everyone within. Second, this informal sphere can later become part of every magical spell or ritual you perform by standing near each token as you formally invoke the quarters. The power of the tokens then mingles with that of the watchtowers, resulting in more potent magical wards.

Last, it allows you to call on protective powers from a specific element/direction as circumstances require. Say, for example, you felt something was threatening your security. You would then use your activating word to mobilize the magical power in the earth/north token, which governs stability, especially with financial matters. Leave this "on" until you feel the threat is past, then use the deactivating word to put the token back into its neutral energy position.

GAIA'S WINDOWSILL GARDENS

**Home is a place where you can catch a dream
and ride it to the end of the line and back.**
—THEO PELLETIER, *Where the Heart Is*

Indoor planters and windowboxes can become miniature sacred spaces that honor the earth. They also provide you with a four-season region where positive energy can always grow toward specific goals. For example, say you decide to plant four small pots with alfalfa, lavender, cactus, and daisy (earth, air, fire, and water, respectively). The seeds for these plants also represent a personal wish that prosperity, peace, protection, and joy will always remain in your home! Once planted and placed in the correct elemental quarter, you activate the living plant's energy and the magic within each time you water it. In addition, such placement creates the informal sacred space previously discussed in "The Elemental Living Space."

Plant windowboxes with similar elemental associations, but this time hang crystals from curtain rods nearby. The plants' growth benefits from the crystals' energy (especially moss agate). The crystal(s) can also be chosen to augment the plant's purpose in your sacred space. Using the previous example, you might hang coal or cat's eye over the alfalfa, blue tourmaline or coral over the lavender, jet or obsidian over the cactus, and amethyst or chrysoprase over the daisies!

An alternative approach to using plants for creating sacred space is that of putting a particular plant or windowbox where its energy will do the most good. For example, a woman wishing to improve physical fertility might keep a decorative fig in the bedroom or place geraniums in the bedroom windowbox. (For more ideas, refer to my book *The Herbal Arts*.) A person whose home needs love and understanding might use a potted dill in the living room and a gardenia in the dining room windowbox.

In all cases, please be certain to use earth-friendly, organic approaches to enriching the soil and managing bugs. Magical energy doesn't always mingle well with commercial products because of unnatural components. These components either taint the results or negate the effort altogether. Of equal importance is the fact that reestablishing sacred space and honoring the earth won't be accomplished by using harmful chemicals.

The concept of making miniature sacred spaces using pots and windowboxes is by no means limited to the home. For example, someone experiencing tension at the office might keep an energized and specially blessed lavender plant at his or her desk. Effectively, this type of thoughtful configuration provides ongoing (and physically growing) support for all of your spiritual goals no matter where you may be.

MAGICKAL MARKINGS

Speaking of portable power centers, I'd like to talk a bit about using subtle markings to establish protected areas where you might not think it was possible before. Say, for example, you've noticed the crime rate around your apartment increasing. How do you make a sacred, safeguarded sphere around an entire city block?

My solution to this and similar situations where you'd like to extend magic to a large urban area is adapted from something animals do all the time. In the wild, animals mark their territory through scent. In an urban setting this translates into using aromatherapy in a whole new way.

Begin by getting yourself some protective oils. Marigold and caraway are particularly good for safeguarding property, and fennel is a good, all-purpose protective aroma. Next, charge the oil by placing it in the light of a waning moon to banish negativity. Afterward, go out and draw a symbol of protection (like the rune Algiz, which looks like a Y with an extended middle line going upward) on every telephone pole, street lamp, and building corner possible using the oil as your figurative pencil.

As you go, visualize white-light energy pouring into these points and connecting each to each. Also, whisper a brief prayer or invocation at each location. When you get home, wrap up the whole ritual by calling the watchtowers to empower and reinforce the wards you just set up. Then each time you pass one of the anointed spots, repeat the prayer or invocation you used in setting up the protected sphere. This reinforces and recharges the magic, helping to maintain the sanctity of your neighborhood.

OUTDOOR ALTARS

**Any time I wish to read the words of God,
the book is before me.**
—ANTHONY OF THE DESERT

Since the earth is the most ancient sacred space that humans have available, nature is perhaps the most appropriate altar for which we could hope. Natural regions, especially those protected from excessive human interference, contain the life-sustaining elemental powers. Here among dew drops, flowers, soil, and wind, the elementals dance and mingle freely. As they swirl and join together, they create an abundance of energy for the Wiccan to call upon.

Our ancestors were certainly aware of this when they created stone or wood altars in the forest, along the banks of a stream, on top of a mountain, or in the middle of the desert. No matter the location, they trusted that the gods were there, inhabiting every corner of creation. Mind you, that was when many more wild places existed. These days you'll have to put a little thought into exactly where to set up an outdoor altar and what tools to leave with it.

To begin, keep in mind your time constraints. Don't put a lot of work into creating a beautiful altar that you never get to visit because it's too far away! Unless you plan to share the altar with others, you'll probably want the area to be fairly private and accessible. If you use an isolated region, mark the way in and out with glow in the dark or reflective tape so you don't risk getting lost at night. Also, make sure that a friend or family member knows how to find this spot in an emergency.

This brings me to an important point: Always make safety a primary consideration. Don't set up an altar adjacent to a cliff's edge, near fast rushing water with slippery embankments, or too close to your ritual fire pit. Also, make sure always to have a first aid kit handy. Why? Because when we worship, our sense of place and time often gets lost. During ecstatic dance, for example, it's quite easy to get bruised or scraped, trip over a root, and the like.

Once you find the right place, the way you build an outdoor altar is just as personal as that for your home, with a few exceptions. First, the altar's construction should be sturdy enough to weather the elements common to your area, as should any housing for your tools. Second, the altar's configuration should somehow reflect its ultimate purpose. For example, an altar that you set up solely to channel earth energies back into the sacred grid need not have human tools on it.

After you're done putting everything in its place, you can then proceed to dedicate and bless the site in a manner suited to your personal path. Take the extra time to invoke the four quarters (and their respective inhabitants), and your god/dess. Welcome both to your sacred site. Despite the fact that outside altars are "in" the elements, elemental powers and the Divine tend to be very respectful of sacred places. They won't usually encroach on one of your own devising unless invited or there's a pressing need.

OUTDOOR GARDENS AND CIRCLES

The Groves were God's first temples.
—WILLIAM CULLEN BRYANT, *A Forest Hymn*

If you have a green thumb and enjoy puttering in the soil, gardening is an excellent medium through which you can create sacred places and power spots. Start by ritually preparing the soil with natural fertilizers, crystals marking the four quarters, small bells to appease the fairy folk, and the like. From here, you can make your garden into a thematic sacred site simply by using a little creativity. For example:

- Plant medicinal herbs in a magical pattern that represents healing so they literally grow with holistic energy.
- Plant four types of flowers (one for each element) in a large circle to create a protected sphere for ritual and spellwork.
- Plant your chosen array in a clockwise spiral, beginning with ground-level vegetation at the outer edge and the tallest in the center. This helps create a positive vortex for nature's

energy to follow (note that a vortex is a natural cone of power for the Witch). If instead, you want to banish a particular type of energy, simply design the spiral so that it swirls counter-clockwise.

- Plant various types of greenery in a mandala pattern, then put a bench in the middle where you can meditate.
- Plant culinary herbs and vegetables in a square garden for strong foundations and security. Put four large stones at the four corners to improve the symbolism.
- Plant vegetation meant solely for magical efforts during a full moon (for the intuitive nature), and lay out the garden in the form of a pentagram.

To expand these ideas into a larger area for a circle or grove doesn't take a lot, other than the resources to plant whatever trees or flowers you want, transport suitable marking stones, and build whatever altar you desire. However, don't just go rolling into an open field and start to work. Sacred sites retain their specialness because of the thoughtful consideration placed therein by the people who design them. This means taking a little extra time and allowing nature to guide your hand.

Look at the way the region is laid out and learn as much about the area as possible. Consider:

- Are there any mountains, streams, ponds, or other landmarks whose spirits you want to honor here, or that could become a central point of the circle or grove? For example, a stone outcropping might indicate a strong earth spirit that could become an ally in your work. This feature might also make a good altar.
- Are there signs of fairy rings or paths that should be respected in the way you set up the site? For example, a ring of mushrooms might be left outside your circle, or carefully

partitioned off so they don't get trampled on during rituals.

- Are there local traditions, myths, or beliefs that could determine or accent this site's theme? For example, say you discover that people believe a particular god or goddess once visited this site. It might be seemly to include a suitable representation of that deity in your plans. You'll see other examples of this throughout part 2, where stories, customs, or religious conviction directly influenced the way a power center was designed.

- Has this site ever been used as a sacred place in the past, and if so can you somehow continue that tradition in your construction? This is very important. Previous use of a site for a specific purpose saturates that region with energy for that purpose. So if you find out that people came to an old oak tree to heal their children, perhaps you could plant healing herbs around its base to honor that custom and keep it alive.

As you plan a sacred site or power center, keep the ultimate goal of your efforts foremost in your mind. It's easy to get distracted by trivials—like having perfect symmetry around the grove or moving an altar an iota to the left. Try not to get too hung up on these kinds of thoughts, which are usually generated by societal training versus spiritual inspiration.

THE SACRED SPACE OF SELF, OTHERS, AND THE EARTH

> . . . Physics now sees the universe as a web
> of dynamic inter-relationships.
> —BEDE GRIFFITHS

In your experiences with finding, making, or working cooperatively with sacred spaces, one binding tie will slowly become vibrantly clear. As the bearer of a divine spark and soul, you are a sacred space; each person, animal and plant is a sacred space unto itself. This means that by staying aware, attuned, and active, each one of us has the capacity to fight against the negative energies that keep people apart and the world despoiled.

Thus, I issue this challenge: Allow your sacredness to reach out to others and the earth; dare to rebuild and revitalize the magical web. One day at a time, one person at a time, one inch of soil at a time, we can make a difference both within and without.

PART II

THE TRAVEL GUIDE

Chapter 4

INTRODUCTION TO THE GUIDE

There are thousands of sacred places and power spots around the world. In a book of this nature, I can only share a handful. In the interest of introducing as many as possible, I've limited this presentation to snapshot portraits. Such brevity can't begin to touch the breadth of a sacred site's significance, all the travel considerations, or all the potential activities you could perform there. It can, however, give you a peek into the timeless human search to comprehend the world's magic, and nudge the inspiration necessary to keep that quest alive.

I've looked to sites across the world and on our own doorsteps in assembling these pages. What resulted was an assortment of countries, scenes, elemental associations, and magical energies that only begins to meet the diversity of human interests and needs. So, if the site you're curious about doesn't appear herein, I suggest thinking about its elemental or thematic associations and finding a suitable alternative location in the index. Or, you might want to research independently, using the texts noted in the bibliography as a starting point.

You'll also notice that many of these places are considered holy to people of one or several other religious persuasions. Why include such sites in a Wiccan collection? For three reasons. First, much of our occult history was driven underground or hidden beneath a Christian veneer for thousands of years. So, many places may indeed have an ancient magical heritage of which chronicled history has remained only partially aware, if at all.

Second, there are many "flavors" of Wicca. What's sacred to a person following a Greek pantheon, someone practicing an Egyptian-styled tradition, a Celtic Witch, or someone involved in shamanic-styled Wicca is, as you would expect, vastly different. So, the easiest way to satisfy everyone was to find the basic theme of each site and provide commonly recognized magical methods for tapping the energy of that theme. From this point, the Wiccan can tweak and adapt the methods to better suit personal tradition!

Third, Wicca is a tolerant belief system that honors each person's path to enlightenment and recognizes the value inherent in human diversity. The world would be a very boring place if each person, and each metaphysical system, was a cookie-cutter image of the other. By touching the energies of a sacred site established by those of other faiths, we begin building bridges from two foundation stones: understanding and an honest admiration for the spiritual sensitivity each site exhibits. Besides, to my thinking, the sacredness and magic of any power center isn't limited by one's religious disposition or the religious preference of its builders; it's driven by the faith, awareness, and respect of all who visit there.

USING THE TRAVEL GUIDE

For reference purposes, the travel guide is set up alphabetically by the name of the site. If you're planning to go to a specific state or country, a cross-referenced list of locations by region may be found in the Regional Appendix.

Each entry includes the location's common name with elemental correspondences and magical themes. If you are looking for a specific place for a special ritual or spell, turn to the Elemental and Topical appendixes, which provide an alphabetical list of elemental correspondences and themes by location, respectively. Note, however, that the magical themes presented here are generalized at best. Many sacred sites were used for a variety of purposes, from worship and healing to social commemoration. Consequently, what I've given are what I consider to be the most predominant influences. But there's a tremendous variety of energies that you could potentially apply at any site so please don't limit your experience or creativity to only what's given here.

The site's location and travel considerations follow. This information is as up-to-date as possible. Even so, it's fairly brief so I suggest contacting a travel agent or tourism authority to help you plan your trip, confirm routing, make reservations, verify room/car availability, and the like. Also, because of changes in everything from weather to the world's political climate, some regions experience fluctuations in how safe or feasible they are for tourism.

Next you'll find a brief description of the area. I apologize that space did not allow for any photographs in this collection, but photographs don't do most sacred sites justice anyway. Read the description and close your eyes. Don't discount the power of your imagination to "see" beyond the words and transport you to another level of awareness. Even when you cannot visit a region in person, let the site and its energy encompass you as you read—let the earth become your spiritual teacher and guide.

Finally, some entries include potential side trips. Regions like Arizona and Greece are powerful vortexes containing several established sacred sites. The side trip notations keep you aware of reasonably close additions or alternatives for travel planning.

Hints for Success

The way a sacred site affects someone is very personal, but there are some helps and hints that will make your experience as spiritually and personally fulfilling as possible.

Travel by Using Your Imagination

- Read about the site's history, background, and description. Get as familiar with the site as possible through images and written word. If possible, also consult other references with imagery.

- Go outside and sit on the ground. Close your eyes, center yourself, and breathe deeply. Think about the fact that the earth is a circle—that this point in reality connects to the one whose energy you need.

- If you wish, create a magic circle in which to meditate and draw the sacred energies of the site to you. I usually recommend this for three reasons. First, you may experience an astral journey during the exercise that follows so you want your body protected. Second, it allows you to call on the specific elemental sphere(s) represented by the site, which can help you connect more intimately with that site. Finally, a protected sphere of magic keeps unwanted presences out of your experience.

- Next, visualize that site in as much detail as possible, then put yourself into the portrait. Dance around the stones; pray to Father Sky; cast spells into the winds; sing with the waters. In other words, see yourself doing exactly what you would most want to do if physically visiting that spot.

- If you feel as if you're flying, your body is numb or tingly, you hear an odd humming sound, or you feel totally liberated from the physical plane, this may signal the start of an astral journey. The confirmation comes when all your senses begin to experience the sacred site's power and presence (in other words, you can hear sounds, smell aromas, feel the wind, etc.). Enjoy it! This is the cheapest form of airfare around.

- Continue with whatever you feel you need to do here. If possible, try to adapt some of the suggested activities in the book to further accentuate the energies. For example, if a suggested activity calls for standing in a waterfall—how about a shower instead?

- When you're done, thank the spirits of the site and the sacred for its help, then return to normal awareness. Make notes of your experience so you can meditate on the meaning later.

Physical Travel: Pre-Trip Considerations

- If you work with an athame regularly in your spellcraft or rituals, check local laws in advance. Find out what size knife is legal to carry (if any), and whether or not it needs to be peacebonded (tied into its sheath). In some cases, in order to keep your athame with you, it may be necessary to get a document from an ordained Wiccan priest or priestess that explains the use of a dagger as a religious implement.

- If you plan to perform a spell at the site, pack components that are earth-friendly (e.g., they won't harm the land or animals in any way).

- If you plan to hold a gathering of any kind on the site, check with the visitors' bureau to make sure it's okay. While it's a wonderful idea to enjoy a magical ritual in beautiful and powerful locations, it's not always appreciated by the locals.

- Pack practically. For example, if you're used to a warm climate, but the site is located in a cooler region, make or borrow a warm ritual robe. Don't negate the transformational power of your experience by getting sick!

- Find some books on the area you'll be visiting and read up on the site before you leave and while you travel. I've found that understanding a site's history, lore, and traditions makes any visit far more meaningful and interesting.
- Don't forget to consult an authority on the area before you go so that your trip is as free from trouble and red tape as possible. This liberates you to focus wholly on matters of spirit and having good old-fashioned fun!
- Don't forget necessities like obtaining proper visas, passports, exchange funds, medicines, and travelers' checks. Again, double-checking these little details will make your trip more enjoyable in the long run.

At the Site

- Go in with an open mind and heart. Doubt and misgivings hinder the chance of having truly meaningful experiences or may initiate negative experiences (see Valley of the Gods).
- Walk gently and reverently. Extend all your senses to the site (think of this like a letter of introduction).
- Try not to expect anything specific, just let the energies greet you. If you anticipate one particular type of experience or sensation, you may miss out on other important things.
- Be patient. Meditate, pray, and wait. Spirit comes to us when our minds and hearts are quiet.
- Be responsive to spirit's leadings. If you feel a sudden urging to follow a particular path, study a tree, or sit on a rock, do so as long as it's safe and allowed, and make sure someone knows where you're going in case of emergency.
- After you've spent some time at the site, consider personalizing the suggested activities in this book or creating your own. This will make your experience wholly unique and better suited to your needs and/or magical goals.

Last, but most important, be considerate of the sacred site. As tempting as it may be, do not randomly take things from the land without asking permission. The walling off of Stonehenge occurred because tourists were literally hacking away at it for souvenirs. Needless to say, we want these sacred places to be around for our children, so if the site doesn't allow trinket gathering, check the nearby gift shop instead.

Also, obey the rules and honor the religious path this site represents. Watch your words and actions so as not to insult the traditions here and the ancient powers behind them. If you think of these spots as open-air churches and treat them with similar respect, you'll do just fine.

Always check local laws, customs, taboos, and tourist bureaus to be certain the activities you undertake are allowable. Always be discreet, law abiding, and respectful of magical places.

Chapter 5

THE SITES

ALGIERS LANDING, NEW ORLEANS, LOUISIANA
Elements: Water, fire
Themes: Peace, passion

Use this as an opportunity to enjoy New Orleans and all it has to offer. I do not, however, recommend traveling during Mardi Gras (two weeks before Ash Wednesday) for two reasons. Airfares tend to be higher, and the mixture of spiritual energies can be somewhat uncomfortable to sensitive individuals.

Alternatives might be Samhain or, if you're a history buff, Battle of New Orleans Day (January 8). Both of these dates have celebrations associated with them that provide plentiful entertainment. In early August there's a seafood feast and the summer concert series at the docks, and in April the French Quarter holds a huge festival accompanied by a jazz extravaganza.

For further information, contact the visitor's bureau at 504-566-5011 or by fax at 504-566-5046 or 5095. They also have a Web site: www.neworleanscvb.com

History and Folklore This particular site is located at the mouth of the Mississippi River near the Gulf of Mexico. History tells us that the land of Algiers was once granted to Bienville, the founder of New Orleans. But that seems to take a backseat

50

to the multicultural appeal of the region, which is a stronghold for the Santerian and Yoruban religions.

The influence of history, custom, and magic is hard to miss throughout the area. For example, for eons, publicly—and today still privately—the Orishas (native spirits) were invoked in Congo Square with ritual, drums, singing, and dancing. Perhaps this tradition and other similar local observances filled with joy and revelry are why New Orleans received the designation of "the city that care forgot."

Locals consider the river the power and "soul" of the city. By putting a flower into the water, you can release a wish directly to the Orishas and know that you will someday return to this place again.

About This Site   There are free ferries available from the Cafe du Monde to Algiers and walkways on the riverfront once you get there. They provide a spectacular view of New Orleans by night, with millions of lights and the sounds of festivities, no matter the time of year. The lake on the other side of New Orleans also adds to the watery energy here.

In terms of fire, something about this area invokes a sense of passion and pleasure. In both the Santerian and Yoruban traditions these feelings are an important, if not essential, part of life's experience. At Carnival this attitude surfaces in abundance, but it's really something that exists year-round, in the way people approach all aspects of life. And, it's a lesson well worth considering.

Activities   As you ride the ferry, offer the water a libation that represents a problem or sorrow in your life, then let the water carry it away. Alternately, whisper your wish to a piece of French bread and drop it into the water spirit as a token. Then either the fish or birds can transport your desire to the gods.

If there's something you've wanted to try, now's the time to free yourself to do so. Enjoy a new type of food, undertake a sporting activity, wear a piece of daring clothing, or whatever. Find your pleasure and your passion here, and experience it to its fullest.

AMARNATH, KASHMIR
Element: Water
Themes: Promises, wisdom, cycles, fecundity, reincarnation

Amarnath is located far to the north in Kashmir. The most convenient city nearby is Srinagar, the summer capital, sitting serenely in the heart of the valley, encompassed by nature's beauty. Throughout the region there are delights for any tourist, including Mughal handcrafts, gardens, and houseboats that you can rent like a hotel room throughout your stay! Srinagar has regular incoming flights from Delhi, for the convenience of international travel.

From here, the first important leg of your journey is but ninety miles away to the east in Pahalgam, a terrific fishing village with a view of Kolahoi glacier. This is also the initiating point for the traditional pilgrimage to Amarnath, a sacred cave about another forty miles away and some 3,800 meters above sea level. The pilgrimage usually takes place the third week in August, July and August being the only months the cave is accessible (with the weather at other times limiting access).

More information can be obtained by calling the India Tourist Office at 212-586-4901, or referring to india. indiagov.org and tourindia.com.

History and Folklore Many Hindu gods live on mountaintops, and this is no exception. Lord Shiva, the god of dance through which all things come into being, is worshiped at Amarnath Cave. Legends claim that Shiva told Parvarti the secret of

creation here. What he didn't know is that two doves overheard his words and, consequently, they can never die. The cave at Amarnath became the birds' eternal home, and to this day pilgrims claim they see doves showing the way to their icy abode.

Another legend tells of the cave's discovery by a Muslim shepherd named Buta Malik who was given some coal by a sadhu. When he got home, he discovered that the sack in which he believed he was carrying coal actually contained gold. Overwhelmed with joy, he tried to find the sadhu to thank him, but uncovered the cave instead. To this day, part of the monies collected from pilgrims go to this shepherd's descendants, the rest being used for the shrine's upkeep.

About This Site   The Kashmir Valley is magnificent, in part because of its rich history filled with people from many different cultures, and in part because the people here managed to maintain their traditions despite many invasions. Even today you'll find vestiges of the remote past in artwork, jewelry, and other crafts.

The Amarnath Cave high above the valley has a unique formation of ice that looks strikingly like the Shiva Lingam, a phallic symbol sacred to Hindus. The size of the ice waxes and wanes with the moon, growing from nothing up to a height of ten feet. At the Lingham's side two other ice figures have formed, that of Parvati, the god of power, charm, and love, and Ganesha, the god of luck.

Activities   On the journey to Amarnath, it's customary to find a walking stick of some sort. This stick is a symbol of personal resolve to finish whatever spiritual quest has brought you here. In the future, it can be used as a ritual wand or a symbol in the sacred symbol of a firm path.

The devout followers of Shiva can receive his blessings here simply by visiting and bearing a gift. Suitable offerings include fasting beforehand; giving bits of turquoise or silken scarves, presenting tiger lilies, rose petals, or geraniums; or burning musk incense. Appropriate requests include gaining wisdom, an awareness of life's cycles, and fertility (especially in men). This is also an excellent site at which to make a promise or vow—to yourself, another, or the gods.

People who have visited here say that it inspires the feeing of oneness with all that has been, and all that will be. Thus, it makes a good location to meditate about your past and future, and balance them out. Release what you no longer need and begin anew, with Shiva's purity and strength as a helpmate. Also, release your fear of death, knowing that Shiva dances in a circle, taking the soul from birth to rebirth.

Side Trips   Try the Bhringi Valley about sixty-five miles away where the Kokernag springs flow with healing power, or visit Delhi for a wealth of Indian history, architecture, and arts.

Angkor Wat, Cambodia
Element: Earth
Themes: The God aspect, leadership, fertility, prosperity

Upon arriving at the main airport in Pochentong you should get a visitor's visa ($20), which requires four photo IDs. Plan to stay in Phnom Penh, the regional capital that also houses the Royal Palace and is known for its visual beauty. Both flights and tours to Angkor Wat may be booked from numerous sites throughout the city. It is also considered a safe city for travelers and has tourist facilities available in a variety of price ranges.

Note that the entrance fees for Angkor Wat tend to be high in order to support the reconstruction of the temples (about $20 per day). Make sure you keep your ticket handy, as you will be asked periodically to show proof of purchase. Guides also run about $20 per day, and they are recommended for both information and safety. Try to come to the area early in the morning for the best spiritual input. For food and temporary accommodations, you can stop in the neighboring town of Siem Reap, a few kilometers away.

Some fun times for travel include October–November for the Water Festival, or late January for the Khmer New Year. More information is available through the Cambodian Embassy at 202-726-7742. A good on-line resource is asiatravel.com/cambinfo.html.

History and Folklore Angkor Wat was uncovered late in the 1800s and is but one of numerous temples in the region, all of which were built between the sixth and thirteenth centuries. Angkor Wat in particular was the cultural and religious center of the Khmer people and has been dubbed one of the world's wonders. Over one hundred edifices dot the region, each glorifying the succession of Khmer kings.

Why so much grandeur for kings? In this civilization a temple was meant to be a symbolic home for the god-kings, and later it became their resting place (a tomb). This particular temple is also sacred to the god Vishnu, so people would often travel here for both rituals and pilgrimages to reconnect with that ancient power. In addition, the mountain into which Angkor Wat was built is said to grant fertility, while the soil brings prosperity.

About This Site   *Angkor Wat* means "city temple," and when you see its size you'll understand why. Spreading out over more than 400 square kilometers, Angkor Wat has suffered from the hands of time, but is nonetheless a true wonder to behold. The symmetry and uniqueness of the temples rival those of Egypt and actually use a volume of stone equal to the great pyramid! The building is surrounded by a moat, and the temple walls are adorned with thousands of sculptures.

Angkor Wat is built into the mountain's face with a temple at the top. The Hindu and Buddhist influences are impossible to miss, the building itself being a symbol of Hindu cosmology. In addition, bas-reliefs on the first level depict some of India's great mythical stories, making Angkor Wat the embodiment of both history and tradition.

Activities   Having been a center that honors the embodiment of god in the form of a leader, Angkor Wat is the perfect location to put a firm foundation under your personal beliefs about god, seek out a patron god figure, meditate about the masculine force of the universe, or recognize the masculine energies within yourself. To enhance the effect, wear an aromatic like patchouli that has strong god vibrations.

To inspire leadership abilities within yourself, try this exercise while looking at the ruins. For it, you'll need a small amount of honey wine, some black tea, an amethyst crystal, and a gold swatch of cloth. Plant the crystal, point-down, in the soil near

Angkor Wat. Pour the honey wine clockwise in a circle around it, concentrating on your intention to tap into the wisdom and strength of the great kings whom this place represents. Next, sprinkle the tea likewise in a circle as a gift to the winds, carrying your wish across this ancient land. Then, finally, gather the crystal dampened by the wine and touched by the tea into the gold cloth (the color of leadership) and carry it with you as a charm.

For continuing productivity and abundance, gather up a pinch of soil from the area and put it in a power pouch or medicine bundle, or place it on your altar when you return home.

ASSISI, ITALY
Element: Earth
Themes: Business success, wisdom, animal kinship

Assisi is located in the Umbrian district of Central Italy. It has several hotels in various price ranges and numerous amenities for travelers. The town also has many sites within wandering distance, including an eleventh-century building that now houses the International Society of Franciscan Studies, a thirteenth-century clock tower, an art gallery, and crafts exhibits.

In terms of travel times, the calendar here is filled to overflowing with historical and religious events, including the Vow Feast (June 22), the Assisi pardon (August 1), and the feast of St. Francis (October 4). If you're a follower of Minerva and have come here for that reason, travel during the spring equinox, her traditional festival time. Or come early in May for the Calendimaggio, a joyful celebration of life, beauty, and fertility that dates back to pagan times but bears Christian influences today.

For more information, refer to www.umbria.org/tourism or call the Italian Travel Office at 212-245-4822.

History and Folklore   Assisi was founded by Umbrian tribes, influenced by Etruscans, and brought to splendor by the ancient Romans. Vestiges of Roman influence are most obvious at the temple dedicated to the goddess Minerva. This Roman deity presided over matters of commerce and industry (e.g., earthly matters), wisdom, the arts, and sometimes also war.

Later in history Assisi established independence as a religious and cultural center (around A.D. 1000). During this period, the town's most famous resident, St. Francis, was born. St. Francis advocated simple living and a close affinity with nature, the residents of which he considered brothers and sisters. In recent years St. Francis's reverence for the earth was commemorated with the World Wide Fund for Nature, convening in the city and specifically seeking to heal ecological injuries.

About This Site   Because Assisi had a multicultural past, it bears that imprint strongly. There are ruins of pagan sacred sites, Roman forums, and Gothic/Byzantine architecture that remain behind as a testament to Assisi's history. The architects of the region were aware of this legacy in everything from archways to houses and doors. In fact, the area looks a lot like a fairy-tale medieval city might have looked, complete with terracotta roofs, city walls, and stonework edifices that turn red when warmed by the sun after a rain shower, then pale again beneath the moonlight!

Activities   Take at least one day to visit the libraries and archives in Assisi, which house numerous hard-to-find texts on religious, historical, and social issues. Also, take a day to hike through the many wooded regions—as you do, it becomes easy see why St. Francis loved nature so much!

From a more magical perspective, Assisi is the perfect location to rededicate yourself to serving the earth in any way you can. Wiccans everywhere recognize our inescapable connection to nature, but in Assisi this realization really comes home to our hearts with Saint Francis's help. By the way, there is no reason you can't petition the Saint for help with this—consider him a kind of guardian or guide on the path to reciprocity.

Alternatively, those people who have Minerva as a patroness, or those who seek her energy for increased secular wisdom and success, would do well to leave an offering at her temple. Suitable gifts include floral-scented incense or any small hand-crafted item that's symbolic of your needs or goals.

AZTALAN, WISCONSIN
Element: Fire
Themes: Summerland rites, offering, power objects

The walled village of Aztalan is located on the Crawfish river in Jefferson County, Wisconsin. Madison is the best place to stay nearby, with its variety of accommodations and amenities, including a botanical garden, boating, fishing, concerts, art galleries, hotels, bed and breakfast facilities, and much more. It's only twenty-five miles from there to Aztalan.

For more information, check the Tourism Department's site at www.tourism.state.wi.us/agencies, or call the Madison Traveler's Bureau at 800-373-6376 (www.visitmadison.com).

History and Folklore   Aztalan was discovered in 1835 and was originally called Ancient City. Unfortunately, nothing was preserved here until after 1912, when the land was locally purchased and designated a park. In 1952, Aztalan finally became a state park, protected by law.

The people originally living in Aztalan were likely farmers who came here because of the rich land in the Mississippi River valley. Over time, some of these people moved up the Rock River into Wisconsin and built Aztalan. Evidence suggests that these people engaged in human sacrifice of some type, likely to honor a sun god. Despite this, it is among the most important archaeological sites in the United States because of the unique ceramic shards found here, tempered out of one shell at a time when most local people were using grit techniques.

This pottery indicates a more advanced system of arts that may have extended into religious worship. There were also stones wrapped in birch bark around the stockade that resemble scrying and power stones in many native traditions.

About This Site   Aztalan consists of three walls, each of which contains flat-topped pyramids, temples, and conical earthwork mounds that have astrological significance and act as markers for weary travelers. The most interesting finding of all here was a beaded woman: a mummy wearing a robe of 1,900 shells surrounded by large natural sculptures of birds, reptiles, and rabbits, which were likely sacred animals. Her spine shows signs of abnormality, which may have elevated her status in society to that of a princess or, more likely, a priestess.

Another unique feature of Aztalan are its fifteen pyramids. The first pyramid resembles the structures of Mesoamerican Indians; the second contained remnants of charred corn, indicating a kind of burnt offering. Pyramid ten has woven rushes on the floor and was part of a crematorium, and the thirteenth contained bodies—one of which had a bundle of five hickory nuts, which was likely a magical charm. Two of the pyramids are dedicated to the sun and moon, respectively, allowing for a diversity of activities here.

Activities   Bring a picture with you to this site of someone who has passed into the next world. At some private moment say your good-byes and wish their spirit well, then burn the picture. Symbolically, this helps release the ties between you and them (other than memory) and urges the spirit to move on to its next reality.

Alternatively, if there's something that you need to figuratively die in your life (a bad habit, old ideas, negativity, etc.), bring a symbol of it and burn it to ashes. Release the ashes to the winds just before dawn, then greet the new day with hope.

Finally, keep your eyes open for a bit of birch bark and a stone that seems to call to you. Gather these and keep them as part of a charm, amulet, power bundle, or whatever. They will provide you with insight into your role as the priest or priestess of your life.

BATH, ENGLAND
Element: Water
Themes: Healing, empathy, emotions

The baths are located near Bath Cathedral, one hour west of Stonehenge and about three hours west of London. Consider staying at bed-and-breakfast establishments. The owners will likely have an abundance of local history and lore for your enjoyment. It is also suggested that you rent a car versus go with a tour group. It affords more privacy, less noise, and less hurried conditions. Summer is an excellent season to travel, as the region has impressive floral displays nearby, specifically in Victoria Park's Botanical Gardens. Late May is also a good time to visit, which is when the festival of Bath—a seventeen-day musical celebration—takes place. This particular event includes children's activities, opera, and art exhibits.

The baths are open to tourists daily. For more information, contact the British Tourist Authority at 800-462-2748 or go to www.britain.com.uk/index.html for on-line information.

History and Folklore The springs in this region are around 7,000 years old. The ancient Celtic inhabitants dedicated the baths to the goddess Sulis, whom the Romans later renamed

as Sulis Minerva and to whom they built a temple that was not rediscovered until 1727.

In Roman tradition people came here—young and old, rich and poor—leaving their sandals outside the pools. They then went to different baths, progressively warmer, cleaning off dirt by using oils rubbed into the skin. As they got clean, people caught up on the news of the day, sang songs, and generally got a reprieve from the day's toils.

The baths were enclosed by the Emperor Vespasian, but before this occurred people used them for worship, healing, and wish magic. One bath, in particular, had over 2,000 coins in it along with engraved stones and precious metals, indicating its use for offerings to the gods.

Bath was once a social center in England, highlighted by a visit from Queen Ann in the 1700s to tour the hot spring baths. This spurred the arrival of numerous influential tourists, ranging from artists to philosophers, from that time forward.

About This Site   The water in the hot springs is likely 10,000 years old, making it truly the water of the ages. The enclosures around the baths are far newer, having been revitalized. They now bear an early-Victorian ambiance. The original cobblestone floors still remain intact. There's a central area for socialization and a specially constructed orchestra vault above.

There are also the remains of a temple here, dedicated to an aspect of Minerva, the goddess of wisdom. The temple comes complete with a giant bronze head of the goddess and several stone figurines. The overall feeling inside these walls is an overwhelming sense of wellness that pours from an ancient power.

Activities   Traditionally, tourists are invited to offer coins to their own particular god or goddess in one of the supplicant pools. The coins that you offer will be used for the future maintenance and upkeep of this sacred site. Or, try running your fingers through the main bath, sensing its warmth and welcoming energy. Let it take away in its comforting drops any negativity or sickness you bear.

If you need more wisdom in your life, leave a small offering for Minerva beneath her statue. Tiger lilies and geranium flowers are particularly favored by her.

Side Trips   If time allows, take a walk down the street to the Abbey, an eighth-century monastery that was later converted into a impressive Romanesque cathedral. The conversion and restoration took place thanks to the efforts of Bishop Oliver King (1500s), who encouraged King Henry the 7th to rejuvenate the Abbey because of a divine vision that linked the king's success with the Abbey's refurbishment.

BIGHORN WHEEL, WYOMING
Element: Earth
Themes: Cycles, healing, accord

The Bighorn Wheel is located high in the Bighorn Mountains on a 9,600-foot-high plateau about thirty miles west of Lovell, the nearest town. Lodging, food, and transportation are available here, and the chamber of commerce can help you with specific questions (307-548-7552). The Wheel is accessible by car by following U.S. Highway 14A, which traverses twenty-five miles of canyon to the national landmark. RVs are not recommended in this area due to steep inclines.

As part of the National Park system, there are numerous facilities throughout the 80 × 30 mile region, including 32 camp grounds, 14 picnic areas, 2 visitors' centers, 2 skiing areas, 2 lakes, and scenic byways. Biking and backpacking are allowed if you take care to "leave no trace," in an effort to keep the area as untouched as possible. More specific details can be obtained by calling the Medicine Wheel District Office at 307-548-6541. Information on camping is available at 800-280-CAMP.

History and Folklore   Historians think that the Plains Indians constructed this earth marking sometime around 1100 A.D., but this date and origin are uncertain at best. The exact purpose of the Wheel is just as elusive. It's suspected to have been a kind of calendar, marking the summer solstice and the rising or setting of certain stars. More than this, however, the image has specific symbolic significance — that of the medicine wheel.

Here, and in many other native settings, the medicine wheel embodies earth's cycles and the order of the universe. When a person dies, his or her soul waits to rejoin the stars underground. The wheel marks the pathway for a person's spirit to follow. Consequently, many local people believe this region is highly haunted.

In addition, the medicine wheel represents each soul's specialness and pathway to spiritual understanding. It embodies harmony, equality, and wholeness. By placing the wheel on the earth and forming it out of natural stone, the natives honored the Earth Mother's nurturing energies and illustrated their beliefs.

About This Site   The Bighorn Wheel is more than 80 feet in diameter and 245 feet around. It has 28 spokes reaching out from a central point, and an external cairn, all constructed from rocky piles. If you stand at the cairn on summer solstice and look toward the horizon, you'll get a spectacular view of the rising sun across the wheel's spokes. The surrounding landscape adds to the stunning effect, with Cloud Peak and Black Tooth Mountain rising 13,000 feet into the air like sentinels.

Activities   Bearing in mind the wheel's symbolism, take a natural token with you (a plain stone is ideal) to leave within the wheel's diameter. Push it down into the soil to plant harmony, equality, and health firmly in your life (or a specific situation). Thank the spirits of the land for keeping the token safe and sharing their energies.

Alternatively, if there's a cycle you're trying to break, meditate on that pattern while walking the circle counterclockwise. This is symbolic of change, decrease, banishing, or turning things around.

Blue Grotto, Capri
Elements: Water and Fire
Themes: Witchcraft, light or color magic, peace

Capri is an island at the tip of the Sorrentine Peninsula. You'll be hard-pressed to find anyone here unfriendly or unhelpful. Capri is well used to visitors and treats them hospitably. You can stay in all types of accommodations around the island, from cottages and villas to resort hotels. For convenience, however, you might want to check into Marina Grande, where boats leave regularly for the grotto. If you're not much of a seafarer, you can also get there by bus from Anacapri.

Note that you cannot see the grotto in bad weather. For more information, refer to www.initaly.com, touristoffice@capri. it, or call: the Italy Travel Office at 212-245-4822 or Capri Information Office in Marina Grande at 39 81 8370634.

History and Folklore   The Greeks were the first to colonize Capri, which probably gets its name from the Greek word *kapros*, meaning "wild boar," the predominant animal inhabiting the island when the Greeks arrived. In 29 B.C. Julius Caesar bought the island from the Greeks because it so captivated his imagination. Legends tell us that his successor, Tiberius, built twelve villas here, dedicating each to one of the twelve gods of Olympus.

The Blue Grotto wasn't discovered in modern times until the first half of the last century, but the Roman statues there indicate a landing spot. Locals knew of the grotto, calling it Gradola, but they stayed away because of stories of in-dwelling witches with pet monsters who protected the magical lair.

About This Site   All of Capri is breathtaking. Its coastline is filled with vibrant cliffs that dip into deep waters and coral reefs, and the land is a veritable garden of flowers, birds, and reptiles. The Blue Grotto personifies Capri's radiance. Here, sunlight pouring through the underwater cavity creates a blue reflection and fills the entire cavern with aquamarine light. The effect is nothing short of spectacular.

Activities   To be honest, it's well worth a trip to the Blue Grotto just to experience its luminescence. The blue water-filtered light generates a peacefulness that cannot be recreated by human invention, and will feel it flowing into and saturating every pore as you stand here. Let that calm fill your heart. Any time you feel out of sync in the future, remembering this moment will help bring things back into focus and restore your serenity.

In some of the caves, particularly Grotta Oscura, water falls from the ceiling as it distills. Gather this in a cotton cloth (or other natural fabric), to absorb the distilled essence of magic and childlike wonder that the area evokes. Use this cloth to wrap special ritual tools or perhaps as a permanent part of your altar.

Side Trips   Some people recommend that you visit Capri for a day tour, using the remainder of your time in the rest of Italy. In the Campania region (southern Italy), in particular, you can go to the oldest Doric temple, located in Paestum, or possibly join a wine-tasting event in Torrecuso. A hike along the coast is very peaceful and invigorating, and Naples (just a short drive from Paestum) has great art exhibits.

One place in particular that you shouldn't miss is Benevento, which holds a Madonna of the Graces festival in July (www.egmit/comuni/benevento). This town can be considered the "Salem of Italy" without the hype. During the Inquisition, the town hosted numerous trials, and people who can trace their lineage to thirteenth- and fourteenth-century covens still worship the old ways here.

Brushwood Campground, Sherman, New York
Elements: Water, earth
Themes: healing, magical heritage (also special events)

Brushwood campground is located just outside of Sherman in Chatauqua County, New York. Take your best route to New York Route 17. Follow this to Sherman (Exit 6). At the end of Main Street, turn left on County Road 15. Follow this for three miles to Bailey Hill Road and turn right. The campsite is one mile down on the left side.

The facilities here include hot showers, flush toilets, a pool, a hot tub, and two covered pavilions for rainy-day activities. The last posted fees for camping were $10 per night, $5.50 for a day visit, or $15 for indoor lodging. Note that merchant fees and spaces are slightly different, depending on the event, so call ahead. Also note that you must register in advance for certain events and festivals, and that during these events the grounds are closed to day visits and nonregistered campers.

There is a kitchen at the facility that will offer food for larger gatherings, and ice and some other daily necessities are also available on-site. Soon there will also be an indoor workshop and gallery area with a coffee bar.

Your travel time will often be dictated by the festival you plan on attending. Know, however, that the nights can get somewhat cold or damp, and/or rainy. Bring a warm blanket and an extra set of clothing. For more information, see their Web site at www.brushwood.com or phone 716-761-6750.

History and Folklore   Brushwood's logo is a leafy branch that blossoms in a heart. This was adapted from an ancient West African glyph called *san kofa*, which translates roughly as "go back and get it." At first, this seems odd until you know the accompanying story.

The proverb says that a bird can't fly if it doesn't tend all its feathers, including the tail feathers. Similarly, people must take care of the past, heal it, and integrate the lessons there, if we are to fly confidently into the future. In addition, it is from our collective past that we can begin to rediscover and reclaim our magical heritage.

About This Site   Brushwood is a rustic, secluded campground on 180 acres of woodland. Many people who visit here for magical festivals jokingly say that the element *must* be water because of the rains and the hot tub. Nonetheless, the grand forest all around certainly sings of earth.

Perhaps the most impressive thing about Brushwood isn't the scenery, although it is lovely; it's the silence! For a while, the pace of life slows down and you're not barraged with noise. This makes Brushwood a perfect location for soul-searching and shamanic quests.

Activities   These will vary according to the gathering you attend, or if you go alone. Throughout the year Brushwood opens its gates to festivals like Heartsong (August), Craftwise in the Woods (July), Sirius Rising (July), and Starwood (July).

Between these events, other smaller workshops take place, including making ritual clothing, designing pottery for sacred bowls and jars, and making paper for your book of shadows!

Note that individuals on a budget can work-barter at events in exchange for their event and camping fee. These positions are few, so contact the folks at Brushwood immediately at brushwood1@aol.com.

Side Trips   Niagara Falls (see later in this book), which is approximately two and a half hours from the site.

CALLANISH, SCOTLAND
Element: Earth, spirit
Themes: Love, commitment, heritage

Central to Lewis Island, north of the Scottish mainland, the best way to get there is via the Stornoway Ferry. If you can afford the extra cost, take your rental car on the ferry. It's a lovely boat ride to the island and the landscape while driving is quietly breathtaking. Just keep your eyes open for stubborn stray sheep!

There are at least two bed-and-breakfast establishments on Lewis, both of which are reasonably priced and within viewing distance of the stone circles. I highly recommend visiting for at least one night. The sight of sunset or sunrise (if it's not raining) is more than worth the price of the stay.

Time your travel for the summer months to avoid the cold, but bring an umbrella as August is particularly rainy. For specific listings of B & B establishments and other travel information, contact the British Tourist Authority at 800-462-2748. Preview maps and photographs of the region at www.stonepages.com.

History and Folklore   Historians estimate that this site was constructed around 2000 B.C. According to local beliefs,

great fires burned at the central circle on May Day, when all other fires on the island were burned out. People then took a coal from the central source (representing spirit and community) to their home to light the hearth.

Some locals claim that the stones are actually druidical guards who can change themselves and move at will. And what do they protect? The ancient resting spot of Myrrdin's dragon, a great spirit-beast who tends all the stone circles throughout the British territories and keeps their energy connected along ley lines.

About This Site Lewis is a farming and sheep-tending island characterized by moors, peat bogs, and low rolling hills that are dotted in spring and summer with fresh heather. Don't expect "fancy" things here; the people live close to the land and simply. Near the East Loch Roag, on top of a small rise, the central ring stands, reaching toward the sky. The energy here is hard to describe. There is a timelessness, a feeling of being part of eternity. You find yourself not wanting to speak or even walk loudly for fear of disrupting the holiness.

Besides Callanish's central circle, which is formed in the shape of a Celtic cross, there are two other small circles to enjoy here, both within walking distance. Unlike Stonehenge, Callanish is not blocked off from public enjoyment. You can sit in the middle of the main circle, touch the stones, and walk the land. Because of this, I don't recommend going with tour groups— they tend to be noisy and to disrupt the sacred energies. From the central circle, specifically, you can take a short walk and look out over the northern seas to touch base with the water element, too!

Activities   According to tradition, this was a place where young couples often declared their vows in the presence of a kindly spirit during the summer solstice. So this is an excellent choice for a honeymoon spot or vow renewal. Stand here with your loved one, and say what's in your heart. Let the stones bless your words.

In addition, many modern students of stone circles believe this region channeled and focused ley line energy, specifically for Druid worship. If you wish to improve your understanding of druidical beliefs or the earth's power lines, this is an excellent place to pray and meditate. Leave a piece of mistletoe (a sacred plant to the Druids) near the main altar stone as a gift to the land and the ancients, and make notes of your experiences.

Side Trips   Scotland is easily traversed by car from one end to the other in under a day, so take in some of the country's other sacred places. While you're up north, take the ferry from Oban to Mull and see Iona, the home to ancient Druids and an area steeped in stories about St. Columba. People still report angelic sightings and miraculous healings here.

Also, stop in Orkney to see the Skara Brae, home to astronomer-priests and the Ring of Brodgar, a large stone circle. Or, turn off in Tayside to see the Stone of Destiny upon which Scottish kings were crowned and where Jacob dreamed of God.

CHACO CANYON, NEW MEXICO
Elements: Fire, earth
Themes: Safety, weather, offerings, luck, creativity, tribe

The best place to stay when seeing the canyon and neighboring sites is Farmington. Here you'll find a golf course, fishing, hiking trails, water sports, amusement parks, and museums to act as diversion between expeditions. Regular tours run from Farmington to Chaco (park telephone 505-786-7014), but there is no public transportation service.

The park is located off NM 57 or NM 44 in northwestern New Mexico, about an hour from Farmington. It offers guided tours, exhibits, and hiking. The visitors center is open from 8–5 daily, and the park remains open until dark. It costs $8 per vehicle for the day and $4 per person. Backcountry hiking requires a permit from a ranger. Camping fees run $10 per night.

Try to travel toward the end of May to enjoy the annual Balloon Festival, or early June for the Aztec Fiesta Days. Temperatures here can vary dramatically, so come prepared for anything from heat to dampness. More information is available at the Farmington Tourist Bureau on the Net: fmncvb@cyberport.com or by phone at 800-448-1240. Or call the New Mexico Division of Tourism at 800-733-6396.

History and Folklore The Anasazi of Chaco Canyon were an advanced people who, when Europe was in the midst of the

Dark Ages, were creating amazing innovations in masonry, irrigation, and road networks. The growth began around A.D. 900 with but one hundred years before Chaco was a recognized economic center for the plateau. Here, various goods, including turquoise, were traded.

It's interesting to note that all the villages along the plateau are closely aligned to the 108th meridian, which could easily indicate a potent ley line. In addition, scientists tell us that the rocks from which the Anasazi built their kivas for sacred ritual show high radioactivity levels, something the shamans may have been sensitive to. Unfortunately, this culture suffered during a prolonged drought, and people slowly started leaving the area, likely becoming integrated with the Hopi, the Pueblo Indians, and Zunis.

Local folklore says that as you travel the roads to Chaco, you should listen closely if a wind arises. This is the spirit of the Anasazi, the "ancient ones," who will whisper a secret in your ear!

About This Site   The best way to see the park is by taking a conducted walk with a ranger. As you walk, you cannot help but marvel at the Anasazi road system, with over 400 miles of traversable land connecting various pueblos. The longest road is over 42 miles and goes toward Farmington. This system is a strong testament to the 3,000 or so people who lived here in its heyday, making world-renowned Cibola pottery and turquoise jewelry.

The ruins themselves also attest to Anasazi creativity. Walls were made out of rubble and shaped stones, slowly building upward to areas over four stories high! Some of these structures were homes, others were observatories, and others still were made to act as calendars.

Activities   The heart of magical activities for this area comes from the turquoise trade that was so abundant and beautiful. The Native Americans used turquoise as an offering to the gods, as part of rain rituals, in medicine bundles, and for protection. Metaphysical applications are similar. Any piece of turquoise you get here can be worn to protect you from accidents and traveling hazards. Or, if you happen to be in New Mexico during a New Moon, carry the stone in your pocket so that wealth, joy, health, and love will soon "rain" upon you. Better still, put the turquoise in your power bundle for continued good fortune.

If you'd like to arouse a little of the Anasazi inventiveness in your own life, simply gather up a pinch of sand somewhere in the canyon (where removal of sand is allowed) and use it later to make a creativity charm for yourself. Augment this by gathering the sand during a waxing moon, so inspiration grows.

Finally, come to the Rinconada, the largest ritual kiva, just before dawn and bring your drum. Greet the sun and Father Sky with sacred rhythms that mirror those in your heart. Connect with the ancient ones who stood here before you and know yourself as part of the human tribe.

Side Trips Go to the Aztec National Monument in Aztec, New Mexico (505-334-6174), just 65 miles north of Chaco. The buildings and ceramics here are similar to those in the canyon, with a 400-room ruin to explore. The entrance fee is $4.00 for adults and the monument offers exhibits, a visitor's center, and various gift items. For more information on this site specifically, contact the Aztec Chamber of Commerce at aztect@cyberport.com.

CIRCLE SANCTUARY, WISCONSIN
Element: Spirit
Themes: Magic, occult studies, ritual, networking

Circle Sanctuary is located in southwestern Wisconsin near Mount Horeb. Advance reservations are necessary for all events or any visit you might wish to undertake. Please don't just show up at the gates, as some events are by necessity private. Monthly events are always advertised and detailed in advance at www.circlesanctuary.org and in *Circle Network News* magazine (Box 219, Mt. Horeb, WI 53572 — $15 annual subscription). You can also call or e-mail for specific information: 608-924-2216; circle@mhtc.net.

If you're coming here for an event, you'll want to stay on-site and enjoy the sanctuary's natural beauty. Otherwise, you can look into bed-and-breakfast accommodations in Mt. Horeb. For general information about travel in Wisconsin, call 800-432-8747 or refer to www.badger.state.wi.us/agencies/tourism.

History and Folklore   Circle Sanctuary was founded in 1974 in Madison, Wisconsin. In the two years that followed, Circle began sponsoring public lectures in the area and educating people about Wiccan and pagan traditions. By the end of 1976, Selena Fox and Jim Alan (the founders) were doing workshops outside the area and forming a coven. But the story certainly doesn't end there.

In the nearly twenty-five years that Circle has served the magical community, their accomplishments are nearly too numerous to cite. They sponsored radio and TV shows, created networking resource books, encouraged intergroup festivals and communications, raised funds for its present headquarters, offered spiritual counseling, began training ministers in the pagan tradition, produced meditation tapes, coordinated events at their site, fought legal misrepresentation and abuses against Wiccans, and published *Circle Network News* — the best-known magical journal in the community. The influence of this organization and sacred site now extends worldwide.

About This Site   Circle Sanctuary is a 200-acre nature preserve that regularly hosts various rites of passage, seasonal festivals, and special gatherings. As one might expect, the residual

energy left behind by so many magical people gathering for festivals and fellowship is pretty amazing. Circle has fought hard to keep its land sacred, to protect the rights of those worshiping here, and to maintain an atmosphere of tolerance and respect. It shows.

Activities   Really, what you do here will depend much on which festival (if any) you attend. If you've made arrangements to visit the land when a festival isn't taking place, use the opportunity for some introspection on your role in the greater magical community. How can you teach about our faith? How can you best represent what Wicca and paganism really are? These questions mirror those that helped found Circle in the first place, and the spirit behind them continues to motivate all that the Sanctuary supports.

Side Trips   Take a trip to the Cave of the Mounds, located just twenty miles west of Madison, off U.S. 151 between Mount Horeb and Blue Mounds. Here you'll find spectacular crystal formations and underground pools. The cave has been designated a National Landmark because it's so beautiful! If you happen to go during summer, you'll also be treated to flower and rock gardens, walking trails, and picnic facilities.

The Cave of the Mounds is open from March until November every day, with guided tours leaving regularly. Parking is free. Call 608-437-3038 for more information or directions.

Copan, Honduras
Elements: Earth, fire
Themes: Calendar, time, mediumship, opening astral doorways

The Copan ruins are located in western Honduras, a country whose name means "depths," thanks to Columbus, who named the country because of the deep waters off the Caribbean coast. The best choice for accommodations are in San Pedro Sula, where the international airport is located. From here you can get tour buses that leave regularly, from early morning to late afternoon, to many sites around the region. Or, contact a local tour operator. Using any other public transportation takes twice as long.

You can also stay in the nearby town of San Jose de Copan, which has a few hotels and a "colonial" appeal. You'll probably want to travel between February and April for the best weather. This timing will allow you to take in the festivities at the Copan Ruins (March 15–20). Alternatively, travel in late June for the annual fair in San Pedro Sula. For more information, contact the Honduras Embassy at 202-966-7701, or refer to either of these two Web sites: www.honduras-resources.com/tourism; and www.honduras.com.

History and Folklore   There is evidence to suggest that Copan was settled as early as 1000 B.C. by Mayans. Between its founding and A.D. 900 a great civilization flourished here, which is evident in the buildings, layout, and artistry. Many of the structures here were used for rites of kingship, while others held special religious significance. In particular, the ball court was used for an annual Mayan ritual in which a ball was kept in the air as long as possible. This created energy that opened a door between the worlds, allowing more magical power in and increasing the priest's ability to commune with spirits.

About This Site   You'll enter the ruins by passing through the town of San Jose de Copan, a tiny but lovely village with cobbled streets and white adobe dwellings. This, along with the naturally relaxed pace of Honduras, sets the perfect tone for the ruins. There are many different areas to see in the ruins, which cover over 300 square kilometers: a stelae that portrays the great rules of the city, a stairway covered in hieroglyphics describing local history, an acropolis with carvings of Copan's kings, and depictions of the various symbols associated with the Mayan calendar.

Activities   The Mayans believed that by carefully adhering to the calendar system they were given, they could reap the blessings of the gods for a good harvest and long life. So, bring your Witch's or lunar calendar with you and bless it at the ruins! Use this in the future for planning any important events so that they go off without a hitch, and reap bountiful pleasure!

Also, if you want to improve your ability to communicate with spirits or improve your awareness of astral energies, this is definitely the site to help you with that goal. One good spell that accentuates this kind of energy entails taking any small, hand-held ball with you to Copan (a crystal ball would be one good choice). Make sure that you keep this off the ground throughout your tour. Periodically, take it out, toss it high into the air, and catch it again. Keep your purpose strongly in mind as you do, then put the ball safely back in your pocket or pack. So doing saturates this object with the same energies the Mayans invoked in their ancient rituals.

Side Trips   Less than a hundred miles away, just over the Guatemalan border, lies Quirigua. This site houses the largest Mayan stela, showing Mayan rulers and animal carvings that represent the Mayan gods. Or, if you're interested in Olmec pieces (some of the earliest Mesoamerican cultures), go to La Democracia, where huge ancient heads and ceremonial masks lie.

DENALI (MOUNT MCKINLEY), ALASKA
Elements: Water, air
Themes: Stopping negativity, cooling fury, protection, energy

Mount McKinley is located in south central Alaska. In terms of travel time, climbers often come in June, which is considered the safest month. However, this can mean crowded local conditions, so you might want to consider July instead. Even then, local accommodations fill up quickly, so make reservations well in advance.

Climbers must register with the Ranger Station sixty days in advance, check in upon arrival, leave no trace of themselves behind, and check out when they leave. For those who simply want to take in the sites, there are numerous guided tours, including air taxis.

There are tourist facilities near the mountain and some camping on-site between May and September, but the best variety of accommodations exists in Fairbanks (120 miles away) and

Anchorage (240 miles away). These two cities and the park are connected by Highway 3. In June, the Midnight Sun Festival takes place, celebrating the solstice. For more information, refer to www.alaska.net or call the Fairbanks Visitor's Bureau 800-327-5774

History and Folklore   In Inuit the word *Denali* means quite simply, and elegantly, "high one." In the late 1800s a prospector renamed the mountain for the current president (McKinley). In recent years a compromise has been reached between the two known designations, calling the National Park Denali and referring to the mountain itself as McKinley.

Native tradition has it that the top of the mountain is inhabited by a solar god who oversees all life. New Agers have reinterpreted this concept as the mountain being a huge power point that collects and redirects mystical energy to where it's most needed.

About This Site   Denali is the highest mountain in North America, reaching upward from the earth to the heavens 20,320 feet. While beautiful and rugged, Denali is also dangerous. At higher elevations people have been flash-frozen to death in the snow, with temperatures regularly dropping to forty below zero. This makes for unique water and earth energy that's moving very slowly.

McKinley represents an impressive challenge for mountain climbers since the timberline ends at 3,000 feet. Nearly 1,000 people try to climb the mountain each year by any one of over thirty routes. For sightseers there's much to take in, considering that the park encompasses over six million acres—moose, bear, sheep, fox, and other animals, along with an amazing variety of habitats because of the mountain's size, are all here waiting for you. There are naturalists on-site to take you on walks and point out the interesting flora and fauna.

Activities   Because of the snow and blustery winds associated with the mountain at higher elevations, Denali is the perfect location to halt or freeze negative energy. Take a natural object that represents the problem you're having and put it in the snow. As ice forms around it, protection forms around you. The ice also sends negativity back to its source like a mirror.

If you've been struggling with anger or ire, the sun spirit here can warm your heart and help you put that bitterness behind. Release your feelings to the snowy cliffs with some flower petals or herbs, look up to the mountain peak, and accept renewal. Turn away and don't look back. That part of your life is now buried and forgotten so you can heal.

Finally, if you know someone or a place that has a great need, implore the sun god here for aid. Raise your hand so you can see the top of Denali between your fingers. Invoke the god and tell him where energy needs to go, then let yourself become a conduit for that power. Feel it pouring down into you, through your feet, and out through the earth to where it's intended.

DEVIL'S TOWER, WYOMING
Elements: Air, earth
Themes: Visions, safety, UFOs

Devil's Tower, better known as the site where part of *Close Encounters of the Third Kind* was filmed, is located in northeastern Wyoming in Crook County off Route 24. Devil's Tower is in a park that offers trails, all types of wildlife, beautiful flowers, a science center, camping, and tours. The monument is open year-round to visitors, with the greatest number of activities being offered from Memorial Day to Labor Day. However, Native Americans worship at the tower during the month of June, so climbers are asked not to venture out during that month. Entry fee is $8.00; $12 per night for camping.

The nearest town, Hulett, Wyoming (307-467-5430, chamber of commerce) is just nine miles away. Hulett is small, hosting an annual rodeo in June and a motorcycle rally in August. It's a great place to stay if you enjoy good fishing, quiet surroundings, and down-home-type people. There are only two hotels here, so you'll want reservations. Sundance is also close, just twenty-seven miles to the northwest and with a few more amenities.

For more information, contact the park (307-467-5283), the State Tourist Bureau at www.state.wy.us/state/tourism, or call 1-800-225-5996.

History and Folklore   Studies of the area indicate that this unique natural feature was likely created by a volcano, the core of which was exposed by erosion from the Belle Fourche River. Since that time Devil's Tower has become a climber's mecca, attracting people from all over the world. Devil's Tower was designated the first National Monument by Teddy Roosevelt in 1906. The name Devil's Tower comes from local Native Americans who sometimes called the region "bad god's tower," which the white man naturally interpreted as the Devil.

The modern native designation is Bear Lodge, which comes from this legend: An Indian tribe camped by the river here, where a large bear population lived. Seven young girls were out playing when a bear began to chase them. The children jumped desperately on a rock and prayed to it to carry them to safety. In response to the prayer, the rock grew upward until the girls were well out of the bear's reach. The bear tried desperately to claw its way up the rock, but it could not follow them. Even so, his claw marks remain, and the girls look down on the earth from their new heavenly abode where they became the seven sisters of the Pleiades.

About This Site   The tower stands on over 1,000 acres, reaching grandly up to the heavens over 865 feet. It's an impressive site, to say the least, but it also has a gentle side, being the home to many deer, prairie dogs, and antelope that are quite used to visitors. All around the tower, pine forests cover the hills, complete with hawks, golden eagles, and falcons.

Activities   This is a traditional site for vision quests and UFO watching, so why not do a little of both? Go out beneath the night sky and look toward the sister Pleiades (also thought to be a region where UFOs may travel from) with the tower in your line of vision. Reach your hands out as if to hold the stars close to you. Pray for vision and an ever-expanding awareness of the universe with all its wonders. Stay there the night, in prayer and meditation, and see what visions come. Make notes of your experience.

Alternatively, gather up a few small pebbles from the tower and keep them safe in a power pouch. The energy in the stones will safeguard you from dangers, especially those in nature.

DRAGON HILLS, GEORGIA
Elements: Earth, water, some fire
Themes: The mysteries, crystal awareness

Dragon Hills is situated in Bowdon, Georgia, on West Highway 5. It is a good hour to an hour-and-a-half drive from the Atlanta Airport, depending on the weather. Because of this distance, it's recommended that you plan to camp on-site, where there are plentiful tent spaces and some areas for RVs.

Dragon Hills hosts festivals regularly, so you'll want to call ahead to see what's up, and when it's best to visit. Their Web site is www.oakgrove.org. Your direct contact here is T'sa: 770-258-9646, or e-mail: dragonhills@oakgrove.org

History and Folklore   Dragon Hills is a tract of private land that has been dedicated to serving the magical community

in any way possible. While I cannot say for certain whether any particular native legends are associated with this area, the locale certainly resonates with an ancientness and power that's unmistakable. This energy is accented by the warmth and hospitality of the Dragon Hills staff, all of whom go out of their way to make everyone feel welcome.

The name "Dragon Hills" says much of what you can expect to experience here. There's a mythic appeal to the land, and you almost expect to see fairies popping out of the trees. In mystical traditions, dragons are intimately connected with the earth and its well-being. They are guardians of ancient wisdom and secrets, and powerful allies in magic. So is this place!

About This Site   I'm not joking when I say this site sparkles. The land lies on a huge quartz deposit. This mound is what I've come to call the Dragon's Back, in keeping with the site name. When paths were put in, bits of crystal were uprooted everywhere. Smaller pieces have worked themselves into the soil, so it glitters in both the sunlight and moonlight!

Dragon Hills consists of 170 wooded acres, about forty acres of which is clothing-optional. The owners have put in many facilities to accommodate gatherings, and there are several designated fire pits (the fire element) for bardic circles, rituals, sacred dancing, or just to join other like-minded folks roasting marshmallows!

Activities   Along the back side of the main part of the property, there's a tiny enchanted creek where you can walk along in solitude. Here the earth and water energies mingle freely. As you wander, listening to the water's secrets, keep your eyes open. I found several very beautiful pieces of milky, clear, and smoky quartz that the land generously provided for my son's collection.

Another rewarding activity to try here is seeking your personal dragon spirit. Dragons exist in astral reality, where they reflect aspects of our personality, act as guardians, and provide guidance. They know the voice of a true seeker when it calls to them with a good cause.

So, come nightfall, find a private spot beneath the stars. Bring with you some type of offering for the land and its spirit—this pleases the dragons. Lay the gift on the ground, then settle your mind, putting aside any other thoughts except what you've come for. Try not to expect anything specific. Dragons can communicate in many ways—through a breath of wind, a spark of fire, the song of rain, or even a wandering creature. Reach out with your spirit to see what awaits you. Don't be surprised if you get mental images rather than physical ones, or if nothing happens but you have startling dreams later. This is quite common.

EAR OF DIONYSIUS, SIRACUSA, SICILY
Elements: Spirit, earth
Theme: Communication

Sicily is the largest island in the Mediterranean and offers warm, but very dry, weather nearly year-round. If you're looking for a specific local festival to enjoy during your stay, travel around January 20 for St. Agatha's festival, which is filled with lights, fireworks, and flowers. The Assumption of Mary (August 15) includes a beautiful boat blessing and giant figurines depicting various portions of local history.

The island has a variety of accommodations, but due to the sporadic water supply you might wish to stay on the mainland and make this a one- or two-day side trip. For seekers wishing to satisfy their stomachs as well as their soul, Sicily is a food-lover's paradise. It is filled with the aromas of cooking pasta, fish, bay leaves, and a heady portion of garlic. Come hungry!

For on-line tourist information, see www.sicilylive.com or call the Italian Government Travel Office at 212-245-4822.

History and Folklore Local lore claims that Michelangelo gave the Ear of Dionysius area its name after seeing the odd shape of the quarry's entrance. Another legend says that the Emperor Dionysius built the chamber in 400 B.C., specifically for holding captives. Dionysius put his prisoners here at night because he could easily hear the echoes of their confessions from outside the cavern. Dionysius also purportedly monitored this region, with the chasm acting as a channel and trumpet, effectively heralding different ideas from around the area direct to the emperor's servants.

About This Site   This is an ancient rock quarry that gets its name from the odd shape of the opening, which reaches 80 feet high and goes back about 250 feet. As you approach the site, gray rock rises out of the ground to surround a cavern that resembles a slightly pointed human ear. The rocks excavated from here may very well have laid the foundations for the Roman amphitheater in the time of Augustus, where Euripides' plays were presented. The result of the excavation was to create a cave of echoes. To this day, if you so much as tear a sheet of paper at the entrance, the sound can be heard even in the remotest part of the cavern.

Most caverns have strong earth-energies because they lie within the soil, in the land itself. In this case, however, I have assigned the predominant element as spirit because of this region's inescapable ties with the sense of hearing, which also affects communication. In this case the message to the visitor is not only to hear, but to really listen.

Activities   Stand outside the cave and meditate on a question that lies heavy on your heart. Close your eyes and just listen. The first words, sounds, or phrases you hear coming from the cave indicate your answer in symbolic or literal form.

In the nearby landscape, find a small gray stone. Take this to the mouth of the cave and bless it in any manner suited to your path. Carry the stone with you as a talisman to improve your ability to discern the truth in what people say.

Side Trips   While on the island you may wish to see Castelluccio, believed to have been constructed between 1800 and 1400 B.C. These extensive rock tombs each received offerings for the spirits of the dead housed there for hundreds of years.

EASTER ISLAND
Elements: Earth, fire
Themes: Stone magic, ecology, harmony

Easter Island sits in the Pacific Ocean, over 2,000 miles away from Chile and Tahiti. The temperatures here rarely exceed 85 degrees, or drop below 57 degrees. The island has a tourist bureau, taxis, bike rentals, and other similar services. Many of the natives run guest houses, which are far more cost-effective and culturally enriching than the island's resorts, but they should be seen first to ensure the quality of the accommodations.

If possible, plan to travel from late January until early February, when you can take in the Polynesian Heritage Festival. More information on this, local culture, money matters, accommodations, and the like is available at these two Web sites: www.netaxs.com/~trance/ and www.entelchile.net/rapanui

History and Folklore   Studies indicate that the first inhabitants here were Polynesians who arrived around A.D. 390 by canoes. At this time, the island was teeming with untouched greenery and birds, which may be why they called it the Navel of the World. Unfortunately, this culture's population outgrew the island in about 400 years. Five hundred more years went by and we find the island's forest despoiled, springs without water, and wildlife decreasing.

Despite this sad tale, the ancient inhabitants were a religious people, building sanctuaries and the great stone statues that are still strewn about the island. Each step of the creation process was a ritual meant to create a holy image, complete with a name that often included the title *ariki*, meaning "chief." More than likely, the finished statues represented kings (ancestor worship is common), spirits, or gods whose immense size was meant to protect and watch over the daily lives of islanders. Some locals still believe these images have a life all their own and can move or travel, if they wish, during the night and return to their exact resting spot by day.

About This Site   The stone statues, known as *moai*, number close to 700 and are scattered liberally around the island. They're made from the lava stone of three volcanos located on the outer corners of the island (fire element). Each statue is over 14 feet tall, some reaching heights of more than 30 feet, making for a rather awe-inspiring site against the native grasses. Many of these have been pushed off their pedestals as part of the social upheaval that took place in the 1800s.

The island features petroglyphs, too, known locally as the talking stones. These are interspersed among the volcanic craters, lava formations, and long stretches of beaches that make for lovely scenery. You'll also find an abundance of native-styled wood carvings and other crafts available at local stores.

Activities   The earth spirit is incredibly strong on Easter Island, partly due to the richness that once was here and partly due to the stone statues. By communing with that spirit, we can rekindle the desire to live in harmony with ourselves, others, and the earth, and also recharge our figurative batteries to help conservation efforts in our own backyard.

The potency of the earth-element makes this an ideal site to carry your personal stones and crystals to. Let them sit on the ground beneath one of the great faces. The base material for most *moai* was taken from the Rano Raraku volcano, making for an underlying but ancient fire element that you can use in directing energizing and cleansing power into the stones.

Also, move yourself into an augmented state of awareness and then look closely with spiritual eyes at the *moai*. You'll find that the faces all look alike, with but minor differences. This mirrors the human soul—each of which has the same divine essence, but small differences that make it truly unique. Let this lesson grow in your heart.

Side Trips If you're traveling via Chile, stop and see the Giant of Atacama, which predates A.D. 1000. This is the largest prehistoric image of a person in the world, measuring 282 feet long. The Giant's companion piece is a carving of what may be a monkey. Both are housed in a ceremonial complex.

ELLORA CAVES, INDIA
Element: Earth
Themes: Creativity, fertility, moon magic, tolerance

Aurangabad is the best place to stay when visiting the Ellora Caves and the neighboring temples of Ajanta. It has a number of attractions besides the caves, including a miniature copy of the Taj Mahal, called Bibi-ka-Maqbara, built in the 1600s, and a water mill called Panchakki where a Sufi saint was buried. Also, because of its convenient location just thirty kilometers away from the caves, Aurangabad has plentiful facilities for weary or hungry travelers and those in need of tourist information, not to mention an airport.

You may want to consider traveling around the third week of March to enjoy the classic dance and music festivals held at the Ellora Caves. Tour buses run regularly from Aurangabad. For more information, contact the India Tourist Office at 800-422-4634, 800-953-9399, or the Indian Embassy at 202-939-7000.

History and Folklore It is estimated that the thirty-four Ellora Caves were used as natural shrines from A.D. 600–100. The Ajantha Caves are older still, twenty-nine in all having been cut in the gorge. Both continue to house some of the finest examples of Indian rock art in the region and are repositories for history and heritage.

Ellora is shaped like a crescent moon to honor the moon god Shiva. For the Hindus, this place gave followers a way to discover their place in the world and the cosmos. Not surprisingly, Hindu hermits often retreated to these caves for spiritual sojourns.

Ellora is best known for its chiseled sculptures, some of which have Buddhist themes. The remaining pieces are of Hindu and Jain origins. This mixture of religious traditions in the caves speaks proudly of ancient India's tolerant attitude toward people with different beliefs—an example well worth following.

About This Site   The paintings in Ajantha recreate the history and lore of Buddhism from 200 B.C. until A.D. 650. The Ellora Caves, by comparison, are filled to overflowing with sculptures that depict, among other things, many Bodhisattvas, people who choose to return to earth to help others rather than move on to enlightenment.

The Kailasantha temple at Ellora, in particular, was made by hand out of one huge basalt rock that resonates with womblike energy. Balancing this, the temple is dedicated to Shiva, the male generative force, making an interesting yin-yang blend. Kailasantha is the largest monolithic structure in the world.

Another site of interest here is the Vishvakarma cave, which depicts dancing, music-making dwarfs. The Jain caves include one with a carved lotus-flower roof and one with a lion under a mango tree.

Activities   If you can get one, I highly recommend buying a *himroo* or *Paithani saree* (loose-fitting wraps) to use in ritual work. These traditionally were made from gold and silver thread woven into silk fabric, making for the perfect balance of sun/moon—yin/yang energies for your magical workings.

Stop for a while at the main hall of the Kailasanatha. Here you'll find the *yoni-linga* that represents Shiva's creative force. In this spot you are at the nucleus of the sanctum, where both Shiva and the Earth Mother resonate with fertile energy. And since most worship was a private matter among Hindus, being alone with your thoughts here to pray or simply absorb the energy seems apt.

Side Trips   Between Bombay and Aurangabad is a town called Nasik. Here you'll find the Godavary River, a sacred site to people of the region, dotted with temples and shrines. The Sita Gupta cave is here as well, where, according to myths, the wife of Rama was carried away by Ravana. Also, just over seventy miles from Aurangabad you can explore the oldest Indian cave temples, the Pitalkhora.

ENCHANTED ROCK, TEXAS
Elements: Earth, air
Themes: Communication, offerings, spiritual guidance

While visiting the Enchanted Rock, located in central Texas, you can stay in Fredricksburg or Llano. Llano's accommodations and attractions are more extensive, featuring many restored buildings from the 1800s, antique shops, bed-and-breakfast facilities, places to rock hunt or bird watch, and many other tourist amenities. Better still, it's quite a pretty 15-to 25-minute drive from the Llano area, along Route 16 to Ranch Road 965, complete with cattle suited to the Texas-ranch style!

The Enchanted Park area can become quite crowded, to the point where they have to limit access, so go early in the day. Fees run $2 per car, or $6 per night for camping. Reservations are highly recommended. In addition, be aware that during

December and January, parts of the park close down to allow for controlled wildlife reduction.

For more information, call the Tourism Division of Texas at 800-452-9292 (www.travel.state.tx.us). For camping reservations call 512-389-8900; the park information number is 800-792-1112 or 915-247-3903.

History and Folklore   Enchanted Rock dates back to the Precambrian Age, making it over six million years old. A tremendous amount of Native American lore surrounds the rock, which is why it's called "enchanted." The top of the mountain displays ghost lights, and the rock itself is filled with an earth spirit that grunts and groans every day (scientifically, this happens when the stone contracts and expands with cooling and heating). The communicative nature of Enchanted Rock is what gives it an underlying air element.

The spirit of Enchanted Rock purportedly helped a conquistador hide from the Tonkawa Indians by extending its magic to the man, and making him one with it. In time, this man became one of the tribe, having been rebirthed by the guardians here into the Tonkawa's keeping.

Today, many students of ley lines claim that Enchanted Rock lies along the same energy path as Ayers Rock (Uluru, Australia) and Tor Hill (England).

About This Site   Enchanted Rock is a huge dome of pink granite that's lovely to look at and great fun for climbers. It's part of a state park that includes campsites, hiking trails, bird-watching areas, picnic areas, and a gift shop. The rock itself rises over 420 feet and covers 640 acres. This represents the United States' second largest batholith!

Please note that the park administration is fairly adamant about protecting the natural and historical resources here. Don't take anything without asking and review the site rules carefully.

Activities It is traditional to feed the rock spirit some type of offering, such as wine or natural tobacco. If your gift makes the spirit happy, it will speak to you and answer a question lying heavily on your heart. Stay in vigil for several hours from noon until early evening and listen for its groaning; open your spiritual ears to understand the words.

To get a stronger feel for the earth-energies here, go to Enchanted Rock Cave. Local stories tell us that more caverns and pathways lie beneath the caves, giving this area the perfect ambiance for introspection. As you uncover the mysteries in your own heart, you will also be communing with the earth's heartbeat that flows throughout the region.

EPHESUS, TURKEY
Element: Water
Themes: Magic, Goddess energy, moon magic

The nearest town to the ruins is Selcuk, which has a number of interesting sites to offer the weary traveler, including a Byzantine citadel and an archaeological museum housing many artifacts from Ephesus's excavations. The other advantage to staying here is that the Temple of Artemis is on the road from Selcuk to Ephesus. Or, you could stay in Sirine (nine kilometers east of Selcuk), which offers nineteenth-century guest houses.

Consider traveling in May for the Ephesus International Festival. For more information, check the Internet at turkey.org or the Embassy of Turkey at 202-659-8200.

History and Folklore Local stories tell us that Ephesus was founded by Androcles. No matter its founder, however, the Classical World regarded Ephesus as a center of the occult arts and magical studies. This is plainly evident by the Temple of

Artemis erected nearby. Artemis was the moon goddess whose other title was "high source of water," which would explain why she presided over traveling weather! Her temple here was one of the seven wonders of the ancient world. Historians relate that the now-destroyed image of Artemis was many-breasted, alluding to fertility, which would explain why women came to her temple for aid in conception. Most important to the Wiccan, however, is her title as the "mistress of magic."

According to legend, the temple originally housed an Asiatic mother goddess whose shrine was built by Amazons over the site of a previous meteorite strike. Later, a Lydian king contributed to its refurbishing, the new wood and marble structure taking over one hundred years to complete. There were also four other temples to the goddess erected here. Later, Ephesus became a Christian center, which led to the destruction of Artemis's temple.

About This Site   This city, which once housed some 300,000 people, is now only a shadow of its former self. The ruins of Ephesus, the best remains of which date back to the third century B.C., cover twenty-five miles, and they glimmer with the beauty and inspiration that must have once existed here. The Arcadian Way, in particular, is a marble avenue over a half mile long, extending like a welcome-way from the port. The surrounding inscriptions tell us that the road was illuminated by night.

If you enter the city from the east and move west, you'll come across Curettes Street, which has fountains, monuments, the Temple of Hadrianus (a god king), and some restored houses with preserved frescoes dating back to A.D. 2. Just to the west of Agora Street, you'll find the Grand Theatre where the apostle Paul gave sermons. This theater is now restored and is still used for folkloric presentations every spring.

Activities   Stand outside as the moon first comes into view over the Temple of Artemis and salute her with a blown kiss.

According to tradition, you should be in the open air to do this—any glass or walls standing between you and the goddess is akin to an insult.

Should you wish to present the goddess with a gift that will entreat her favor on your lunar-empowered spells, you have several options. Bear images, quartz, moonstone, pearls, mandrake, almonds, hazel, jasmine incense, and aloe juice are all sacred to her. Pick one or a combination that you feel most suited to your needs and put it in the earth near the temple, with a prayer of thankfulness.

Side Trips Take several days in Izmir, known as the Pearl of the Aegean. It's the third largest city in Turkey, offering fishing, woodlands, olive groves, long pristine beaches, parks, many fine hotels, dining facilities, shopping, and a mild climate. Here you'll find the Balcova Thermal Springs, which have therapeutic value, and a bird sanctuary for hundreds of types of birds.

EVEREST, TIBET
Element: Spirit
Themes: Sacred song and dance, luck

Mount Everest is located along the Tibet-Nepal border in Sagaramatha National Park and the Qomolangma Nature Preserve. While you can access the mountain from either country, I've chosen the Tibetan tour to honor the Dalai Lama and his struggles. Unfortunately, because of political upheaval, it will be necessary to travel with an organized group that can obtain special permits from the Tourist Bureau.

The best choices for accommodations in Tibet are found in Lhasa, the political and spiritual capital of the region. The city offers all levels of hotels, eateries, sites, and activities to fill your free hours. The best time to travel is from March to October.

Regular flights are available between Lhasa and Kathmandu, to access the mountain more easily and quickly than by road. However, buses are available for tours along the Lhasa highway and donkey walks are available through the city.

Call the Tourist Bureau of Tibet at 011-86-891-34632. Other good resources include: the China International Travel Service at 415-362-7477, the India Tourist Office at 212-586-4901, or the Nepal Embassy at 202-667-4550

History and Folklore   Known as the place where "earth meets the sky," Mount Everest is approximately 60 million years old. The word *Sagaramatha* means "mother of the universe." These two designations combined give the whole area strong connections with the Sacred Powers of all creation and a time-lessness that's inescapable.

The entire area around Everest is inhabited by the Sherpa people, an agricultural group who came here around the 1500s, carrying their Buddhist beliefs with them. In recent years the

Tibetan side of Everest has become a nature preserve and a restoration region for various Buddhist sites, tools, and sacred texts.

About This Site   Tibet is the largest and highest plateau in the world, which is why it got the designation "roof of the world." Similarly, Lhasa is called the City of the Sun because of its altitude, which reaches to 3,600 meters. Mount Everest itself is 9,700 meters above sea level and is known natively as Mount Qomolangma.

Rising bravely above the surrounding craggy rocks, rivers, and glaciers, Mount Everest has a mix of climates that mingles all the elements together into a powerful blend. Everything from a forest to an arctic zone exists here, surrounded by clouds and sky.

In the summer months all manner of plants burst from its hillsides, accompanied in the air by colorful butterflies that seem to dance in celebration of life. Numerous endangered animals live here, so take care to respect the rules of the area and leave nothing of yourself behind but good wishes.

Activity   Tibet is sometimes called the sea of song and dance, alluding to the celebratory manner in which people here approach life. So, even if the only private place you can find is the hotel room, use it and perform a favorite sacred song and dance of your own. Reach your hands up toward the heavens like the mountains that surround you, and let your spirit become one with the sky!

A charming local custom says that if you wish to give someone good luck, pass along a colorful silk scarf. So, buy plenty of these for gifts while you're sightseeing!

Side Trips   While in Lhasa, take the opportunity to visit the Potala Palace, the seventeenth-century winter residence of the Dalai Lama, and Jokhang Temple, which houses the golden statue of Buddha Sakyamuni.

EVERGLADES, FLORIDA
Elements: Water, earth
Themes: Ecology, primal energy, beginnings,
   the mysteries

About twenty minutes south of Miami, the Everglades begin stretching out over 1,500,000 acres. From Miami, follow Route 821 (the Florida Turnpike) south to Florida City. Turn right on Palm Drive (the first light) and follow the signs to the park. From other parts of Florida, the Everglades are readily accessible off U.S. 41.

The best time for travel is between December and April, when the temperatures are more comfortable. If you have to travel in the summer months, come ready for rain and mosquitos. Besides its beauty, the park and neighboring areas offer numerous activities for the outdoorsy person—boating, fishing, hiking, camping, area tours, boat tours, canoeing, and animal exhibits. Park admission runs $10 per car or $5 per pedestrian/bike at the main gate. Passes can be obtained for $20, which will allow you into all the facilities.

You have several choices of accommodations. On-site is the Flamingo Lodge, which has over 100 rooms and 24 cottages. The phone number there is 1-800-600-3813. If this is booked up, you might want to look into Everglades City (20 miles south of Miami) for restaurants, small hotels, and bed-and-breakfast facilities. Otherwise, the next best bet is Miami for an abundance of options.

For further information, contact the Everglades National Park 305-242-7700, the Miami Travel and Transportation Board at miamibeaches.com (800-933-8448), the Everglades City Chamber of Commerce at florida-everglades.com (800-753-8448), or the National Park Service at nps.gove/ever.

History and Folklore   In various metaphysical traditions the alligator/crocodile, which is a famous resident of the Everglades, represents the primordial mother who acts as a protectress of ancient knowledge, a rain-bringer, and a creature who sometimes carries souls to the next life. Carrying an alligator tooth will protect you from witchcraft, wounds, and pain.

As for the Everglades themselves, in 1996 a committee was created to begin an environmental investigation into the importance of the Everglades as an ecosystem and to find effective means to protect it. Presently, there are four National Wildlife Refuges here and one Marine Sanctuary.

About This Site   One cannot go to the Everglades without feeling that one has arrived in another time — a land from humankind's remote past when wilderness ruled supreme. This is the largest remaining subtropical region in the Continental United States with both fresh and saltwater regions. It is one of the few areas where both alligators and crocodiles live together.

The Everglades National Park has five visitors' centers, each of which hosts specific attractions. At the Ernest F. Coe Center (8–5 daily, near the main park entrance) you'll find educational information on the ecosystem, general necessities, and souvenirs. At the Royal Palm Center (4 miles west of the gate, open 8–4) there are more displays and the beginning of two hiking trails. Flamingo Center is 38 miles southwest from the main gate (7:30–5:00) and is a more complete visitor's center with a marina, canoe rentals, a post office, and teaming wildlife to fill your vision at every turn. From Gulfcoast Center (in Everglades City proper) you can explore the 10,000 islands where manatee, osprey, and dolphins live. Shark Valley Center is on the northern edge of the park and is part of the "river of grass," a 100-mile line of marshland and tree islands. This is the best place for alligator sightings.

Activities   Find a safe place away from the crowds (please pay attention to posted areas). Sit and meditate quietly. Listen to the wilderness around you, and know its voice as part of humankind's ancient tribal past. Look within yourself and find the wild person who still exists there, with keen senses and instincts like that of an animal. Smell the air, feel the humidity on your skin, hear your wild brothers and sisters all around— reunite with that primal force and let it energize your spirit.

If you find any alligator teeth at approved souvenir shops, you might want to get a tooth for yourself and wear it whenever you feel the need for safety or increased goddess awareness. Dip this in water and sprinkle it around when you want to invoke rain.

Finally, gather a little water from this area, bless it, and keep it in an air-tight container. You can use this as a component in spells as a way of empowering the start of a new effort, of encouraging fertility, for earth-healing efforts, or for any ritual designed to increase your awareness of the mysteries.

Side Trips   Several possibilities exist. The first is Big Cypress National Preserve in Ochopee, Florida. This park covers 720,000 acres and offers trails, environmental education, ranger-led wetland walks, and convenient camping; it is within a stone's throw of the Everglades National Park (specifically, the Shark Valley entrance). Call 941-695-4111 for more information.

Second, take a commuter flight to Orlando (or a car) and visit Walt Disney World. It is a Mecca for the child within all of us, and as the "magic kingdom" it certainly belongs in any Wiccan collection of sacred sites! All the travel information you need for Disney is available on-line at www.disney.com.

EXTERNSTEIN, GERMANY
Elements: Earth, water
Themes: Dragons, initiation, chakras, the Goddess

Also called the Dragon Stones, the site of Externstein, Germany, is located just south of Detmold, and thirty miles southwest of Hannover. You can find accommodations in Detmold, including a Sheraton Hotel, but Hannover has a greater variety.

Please note that Externstein is one of the most popular tourist attractions in the region because of its incomparable beauty. It's best to arrive early in the morning (before 10 A.M.) if you don't want to be surrounded by hundreds of other people. Night visits can be quite lovely, too. For more information, refer to www.germany-tourism.de

History and Folklore   In Externstein's earliest recorded history it was always used as a place of learning and worship. Here, seekers came to seek initiation into the mysteries, during which time they would undergo three days of isolation meant to inspire spiritual or visionary dreams. With this in mind, it's not surprising to learn that this site was mentioned as central to numerous heroic tales and that it once housed many religious people.

Up until the eighth century the Irmensul, the German version of the World Tree, was rooted here, but it was tragically cut down by Charlemagne. In shamanism the World Tree is a point of astral travel, for the cabbalist it is the Tree of Life, and for Wiccans it is a microcosm of the cosmos and our threefold nature.

In the 1920s the site became more popular as a sacred place, believed to be linked by ley lines to others in northern Germany. According to modern experts on earth-energies, Externstein is the root-chakra of the area and a geomantic center, from which magical energy flows through all its surroundings.

About This Site   Cradled in the heart of the ancient Teutoburger Forest and raising its head over 125 feet above the trees as if to take a peek, this outdoor temple is an interesting mixture of human fashioning and nature's hand. Lir.estone rocks create the backdrop to which various features have been added throughout Externstein's history. Among these additions is a chapel/observatory formed out of rock with a window that faces the moon in its northernmost point and the sun at summer solstice.

A pagan site for thousands of years, the site has carvings at the top of a spire, indicating that it was a temple, possibly created by Romans to honor Mithras or possibly a housing for the Veleda, the German prophetesses. Christians made good use of nature's handiwork here, too. In the twelfth century a huge relief of Christ being lifted from the cross was cleaved out of a large rock.

Activities   The ancient pagans regarded this region as a perfect spot for accessing the power of the Mother and of Dragonkind. If you have contemplated dedicating yourself to a particular goddess, if you wish to connect with goddess energy, or want to seek the counsel of dragons, this is the place to start.

There are several stopping spots that represent other chakras along the way, where spiritual seekers can stop and meditate about the meaning of each power point in the land and in themselves. The crown chakra begins five miles away at a statue of St. Michael near Detmold, which commemorates a victorious battle. Then there's solar plexus mountain, and a heart-chakra hill near a bird sanctuary. Exactly what these places mean to you will depend on how you interpret the chakras and how ready you are to experience the transformation that comes with opening yourself to this energy. To help prepare, you might want to take a trip over to Bad Pyrmont beforehand, a small town with mineral springs that are traditionally used for cleansing and centering yourself.

FUJIAMA, JAPAN
Element: Spirit
Themes: Cleansing, worship, astral travel, energy

Mount Fuji lies just southwest of Tokyo, and there's plenty of public transportation available into the region from almost every point in Japan. One of the most beautiful resort areas to consider is the Fuji Five Lakes, from which you can often see the reflection of the whole mountain on the crystal blue waters. Or you might stay in Suruga Bay and take boat tours along the coast. If you decide to stay in Tokyo, it will take a little over three hours to reach the site. Climbers might want to stay in Fujiyoshida City, which has a climbing trail that ends at Fuji's summit.

In terms of timing your visit, the traditional climbing season here is July and August, which makes for very crowded conditions. On a more positive note, the Fire Festival (Yoshida no Hmatsuri) takes place in late August and is an experience well worth fighting the masses to see. Anyone watching the sacred flames will be purified and cleansed. As an alternative, travel in mid-April to enjoy the blossoming of cherry trees and azaleas, which herald spring's arrival with amazing beauty.

For more information on-line, see www.jnto.go.jp. Or call the Japan National Tourist Organization at 212-757-5640, the International Affairs Desk at 81-555-24-1236, or Tourism Promotion Subsection at 81-555-22-1111, ext. 405. This last organization has maps, brochures, pamphlets, and event information readily available for tourists.

History and Folklore   Mount Fuji bears the name of an ancient Ainu fire goddess who also presided over all household matters. So it's not surprising to discover that the mountain has been worshiped by humans for thousands of years. In folklore it is sometimes called the "mountain nearest heaven." Since the entire world for the ancient Japanese was encompassed by China, Japan, and India, this designation seems apt.

Mount Fuji is a relatively young volcano that last erupted in 1707 (the fire element). Its visual impact has repeatedly inspired writers and artists to the point that it has become the symbol of Japan itself and is regarded as a national treasure.

About This Site   Mount Fuji is the highest peak in Japan (the air element), reaching a height of 12,380 feet. In comparison to the surrounding valleys, the mountain seems to touch the heavens with a unique nobility. Its nearly flawless symmetry combines with the surrounding lakes (the water element) to make for an amazing photographic presence.

Although she has remained quiet for three hundred years, she is far from being "dead." The earth's blood and goddess energy are still quite alive here. The mountain's personality even changes with the seasons and times of the day. If you visit in summer, you'll see a bluish mound wearing a stylish white hat, whereas in winter she's adorned totally in white. When the sun sets, the mountain seems alive again with fire.

Activities   If you go during climbing season, time an excursion so that you can see the sun rise above the clouds at the seventh or eighth station noted on the trail. I guarantee you'll never forget the brisk air as the sun ignites it with life, and so, too, your spirit! There's also a shrine along the way where you can obtain a lovely calligraphic stamp, and if you're feeling really "airy" you can reach out and touch someone by calling them on the phone located on the mountain!

From a more spiritual perspective, Mount Fuji represents nature's soul, and since the mountain is 600,000 years old, that soul is wise and powerful. From this place you can leave your body and travel the gateway to other realms. With the numerous shrines and gardens dot the region, you should have little trouble finding a semblance of privacy.

Side Trips   Near Fujiyoshida you can see the shrine of Kitaguchi Honu Fuji Shengen Jinja. A favored shrine of Japanese warlords, the entrance to the shrine is lit by stone lanterns and protected by a Zuijinmon gate that wards off malicious spirits. The site was originally dedicated to the goddess of Fuji, also known locally as Konohanasakuya-hime or Sengen-Sama.

Within the shire there's a special area for prayer, one for music and dance, and another still for purifying oneself in the mountain's natural spring water before worship.

If you've come all this way, it's also well worth venturing down into the Osaka region and seeing the Ise Shrine and Horyuji Temple. Ise is the most important Shinto shrine in Japan, being dedicated to the sun goddess Amaterasu. Every twenty years people disassemble the shrine and build it anew to represent ongoing restoration and rejuvenation in nature. Ise houses the sacred mirror that once helped bring the goddess's light back to the world. The inner shrine is dedicated to a harvest goddess, and two rocks nearby, *meota iwa*, are said to be the embodiment of powerful spirits who gave birth to all things.

Horyuji is equally steeped in tradition, being one of the oldest Buddhist temples in Japan. This site includes a five-story pagoda and sculptures portraying Buddha's life. It's located in the town of Nara, where you'll get to see many wonderful representations of the Buddha, all of which will have offerings before them—a tribute to the devotion of the Japanese people.

GANGES RIVER, INDIA (BENGAL AND BANGLADESH)
Element: Water
Themes: Purification, providence

The mouth of the great Ganges River empties into the Bay of Bengal between Bengal and Bangladesh, and just bordering on Burma. Probably the best choice for accommodations is in Varanasi, also called the City of the Holy Ganges. Varanasi is one hour by air from Delhi, its airport is only about twenty minutes away from hotels and eateries, and it has numerous tourist facilities in a variety of price ranges. Here you'll get to see the Durga Temple with a golden bell that worshipers ring upon entering to greet god and *ghe ghats*, huge stairs that pilgrims follow down to the river to bathe.

Two alternative cities to stay in at the beginning or end of your travels are Dhaka Bangladesh or Calcutta Bengal. Staying in Bangladesh provides convenient access to two other sites, Mainimati (see "Side Trips") and Bagerhat, the resting place of the great Sufi mystic Khan Jahan. I mention the second one because mosques dedicated to Jahan dot the entire region. On the other hand, Calcutta seems to have a better assortment of amenities and services for travelers.

For more information, contact the Bangladesh Embassy at 212-342-8372, the India Tourist Office at 800-422-4634, or the India Embassy at 212-939-7000.

History and Folklore   Both Ganges and Varanasi have a tremendous wealth of history and lore associated with them. Beginning with the city itself, if a person dies here it's said that they go straight to Nirvana (heaven). The city is sacred to Shiva and dedicated to his worship, because the god was said to have lived here during a lifetime.

The Ganges River balances the male energy with the presence of Ganga, a cleansing mistress who washes away sin and inequity. Every spring Ganga is considered reborn, during which time she is also the goddess of food and providence.

About This Site   The Ganges River is one of the greatest in the world, flowing well over 1,500 miles from its source in the highest mountains through the heart of numerous countries. It is nearly impossible to stop anywhere along the Ganges's course and not find everything from a small hand-made altar to full-blown religious ruins.

Activities   Consider reciting the beautiful invocation of the Hindu people, or an adaptation thereto. Repeat the prayer inwardly or outwardly at this goddess' shore:

"Mother Ganga, may your water—abundant blessing of this world, treasure of Lord Shiva, playful lord of all the earth, the essence of the scriptures and the embodied goddess of the gods—may your water, the sublime wine of immortality, soothe my troubled soul."

To this I would respectfully add, "and make me whole." If you wish, leave Ganga a gift of a water bottle, a lotus blossom, or fish.

Alternatively, you can change the invocation to one that honors the universal goddess figure. Here's an example:

"Mother of the universe, from whom blessings flow, Maiden of all bounty and joy—consort, helpmate, and lover to god—the Crone of wisdom and learning, may your waters, the essence of moonlight and intuition, soothe my restless spirit, and inspire my soul."

Side Trips   In Chittagong, Bangladesh, you can visit the Mainimati ruins, created between the seventh and twelfth century A.D. These ruins mark the center of Buddhist culture for hundreds of years. In particular, Koltila Mura stupas represent the three jewels of Buddhism, with the central stupa shaped like the wheel of dharma (universal law).

In Bihar, India, you can visit the seventh-century site of one of the world's great universities, Nalanda, as well as the Bodh Gaya, a temple that houses a direct descendent of the Bo-Tree under which Buddha attained enlightenment. These three places are all within 300 miles of one another, the last two are only 150 miles from Kathmandu and within a stone's throw of Varanasi.

PYRAMID OF GIZA (KHUFU), EGYPT
Elements: Fire, spirit
Themes: Universal awareness, reincarnation

Located in Giza, Egypt, near to the necropolis of Memphis and part of modern-day Cairo. There is plenty of lodging in Cairo. Or, you could book a room at the Mena House Oberoi Hotel, twenty minutes outside of Cairo, which is adjacent to the pyra-

mid itself. This hotel has impressive gardens, antique collections, and a full display of art to keep you busy when you're not exploring other sites.

One potential time to travel is around September 11, the Coptic New Year. This is when Sirius shines in the Egyptian sky to announce the flooding of the Nile and a season of abundance. For more information, contact the Egyptian Tourist Authority at 312-280-4666. For on-line information, refer to www.its-idsc.gov.eg/tourism/docs/cairo

History and Folklore Considered one of the Seven Ancient Wonders of the world, this monument was constructed by Pharaoh Khufu around 2506 B.C. as his burial tomb. In Greece he was known by the name Cheops and ruled for over twenty years, which was a good thing. Historians believe it took twenty years to create the pyramid, even though they can't be sure exactly how it was done!

The Great Pyramid is constructed from over two million blocks of limestone and granite, each of which weighs a minimum of two tons. It reaches upward of 450 feet and covers an area close to seven city blocks on each side. Despite these generous proportions, people prone to claustrophobia will find the interior somewhat stifling.

Modern beliefs about this pyramid and others like it vary. Some say it was a place where the rulers prepared for their next incarnation, others consider it a temple, while others still claim it's a type of observatory, or perhaps a structure designed by ancient astronauts. One interesting observation came to light recently when comparing the three pyramids at Giza to the Belt of Orion. The arrangement was the same, which might mean that Giza was created as the earthly home for Osiris, the god associated with that constellation in Egyptian astrology.

About This Site   An ancient Arabic proverb says "man fears time; time fears the pyramids." When looking at the strength and size of this ancient structure, one cannot help but feel similarly. This pyramid is the largest single building ever made. It rests in a blanket of sand and stone, jutting upward like a pointer to the sun. The north face of Giza houses the entrance, with corridors, galleries, and the walkways to the burial chamber. Here the sarcophagus is oriented with the directions, likely due to superstitions about how a body had to rest to ensure the spirit's return and safety in the next life.

A bonus to visiting Giza is that several other pyramids and the Sphinx are nearby, along with a museum that contains the Sun Boat found in the Great Pyramid. This is the boat that was to be used to take Khufu on his journey to the other world.

Activities   With so much sand around, take a little bark home with you for those times when you want to connect with the energy of fire. Hold this in your hand and sense all the people and history these grains have seen. Welcome the warmth and protection of the Egyptian sun god, Ra, embodied by the sand. Carry this with you in a special container as a shielding amulet. If possible, mark the container with an eye, which is Ra's symbol.

At night, take the time to look at the sky above Giza and see how the pyramid seems to beckon to it. Consider your place as a citizen of eternity and the universe itself, and let the energies here carry you where they will astrally.

Side Trips   If time allows, take a trip down the Nile to just outside of Aswan and see the Abu Simbel temple with its four statues of Ramses, over 65 feet tall. In addition, the figures of Ptah, Amun, and Re-Harakhty are here waiting for Ra's sunlight, which shines on them every February and October 22.

A shorter jaunt (200 miles versus 300) in the same direction will land you near Luxor, where you can take in the sacred sites of Abydos and Dendra. Abydos was Egypt's funerary center, and it houses a Temple of Osiris, the god of the underworld. Dendra, by contrast, has the remains of Hawthor's Temple, the goddess of fertility (life's continuance) and the sky.

GLASTONBURY, ENGLAND
Element: Earth
Themes: Earth magic, the Goddess, fairies, miracles

Glastonbury is set along the southwestern coast of the United Kingdom. As with most destinations in England, the town offers at least twenty bed-and-breakfast accommodations, which is by far the best and most enriching way to see the country and learn its stories.

Annual pilgrimages to Glastonbury, following in Joseph of Arimathea's footsteps, take place in June. For Wiccans, however, I recommend May Day—a time to rejoice in earth's reawakening and, like the Glastonbury Thorn, find ourselves likewise reborn. More information can be obtained on-line at www.britain.com.uk, or www. visitbritain.com. Or call the British Tourism Authority at 800-462-2748.

History and Folklore In its most ancient history, the peak of the Tor was the home to Gwyn ap Nudd, a lord of spirits. He later became the fairy king, and the lands under his protection became sacred pagan sites.

Epics also tell us that Joseph of Arimathea founded Glastonbury by thrusting his thorn staff into the ground, from which sprang a tree that flowers in spring and Yule. It was here that Joseph purportedly hid the Grail. While known to most as the Cup of Christ, for pagans the Grail has far older roots in the druidical traditions as representing our inescapable connection to the earth. For the Druids, the Grail was the Cauldron of Cerridiven, representing the Goddess' womb from which we are reborn after death.

There is a good chance the Glastonbury Abbey was built on the site of earlier earth-goddess worship. And, in Glastonbury Tor, monks are said to have uncovered the gravesite of the legendary King Arthur. When the Abbey was closed in the 1500s, the monks apparently hid all its treasures in tunnels beneath the site. When people are ready to learn the secrets these treasures contain, the way into the underground caverns will be revealed.

About This Site In New Age terms, Glastonbury represents an important energy center that speaks to the heart of all it is to be human. Here we find the mingling of pagan, Druid, and Christian beliefs, along with history and legend, which makes for a truly rich journey. Going to Glastonbury is, for many people, like coming home and finding that what they sought was really there all along.

Looking at the site from a distance away, the Abbey is unmistakeable: a tall tower atop a summit against a nearly flat landscape. Because of the valleys all around, the Tor is often surrounded by fog, making it look as if it stands in another time filled with the memories of fairies, princesses, and wondrous beasts.

Activities   Many visitors report sighting small balls of colored light dancing around the Tor. While some might consider this a kind of St. Elmo's Fire or Will-o-the-Wisp, I feel they're a physical representation of the ancient devic powers that live in this land. To experience these, spend a night sleeping near the Tor or, if allowed, in the tower itself. Before you go to sleep, leave out a small offering of honeyed bread or cream for the nature spirits, and pray that your psychic insights will be keen. Following this procedure often results in a spiritually revealing dream or an encounter with the fey.

Side Trips   Under fifty miles away to the east you can go visit what is perhaps the most famous sacred site in the world: Stonehenge. Likely used for ritual and worship by the druids, priests of nature, the site also has strong astrological correlations, alluding to its being a type of stone calendar to mark the seasons.

HALEAKALA NATIONAL PARK, HAWAII
Element: Fire
**Themes: Sun and star magic, balance, compromise,
   soul gazing**

Haleakala is located on the eastern point of the island of Maui and is accessible by Highway 36, or Highway 31 if the rains aren't too heavy. It is approximately ninety miles away from the Wailea and Kaanapali resorts, and about sixty miles away from central Maui. Maui has no public transportation so you'll need a vehicle or to make reservations for a tour. Weather can vary a lot in this region, so it's suggested that you pack clothing that can be layered and an umbrella so you can adjust accordingly.

In terms of travel times, Aloha Week Festivals take place during September or October with an abundance of pageantry. The parades alone are a feast for your eyes. For further information and some regional pictures, refer to this Web site: www.us-national-parks.net/hale/info.htm. Or, call the visitor's bureau at 808-923-1811.

History and Folklore   Haleakala is a million-year-old volcano that has been dormant for two hundred years. The cool sides are streaked with red and yellow hues from the minerals deposited there, giving even more significance to its name. Haleakala means "house of the sun," and the coloring certainly adds to that effect, especially at sunrise, when the mouth of the crater glows like amber.

Legends tell us that this is where the sun began each day's journey. Then, for some reason, the sun got lazy and started racing across the sky. As a result, the crops didn't ripen and people didn't have enough time to work. The clever trickster Maui had a solution. He tied sixteen ropes to the sun to slow it down. Even then, the sun was not content. So, Maui struck a deal with the sun. They agreed that the sun would race across the sky for six months (winter) and move slowly for six months (summer) to create balance.

Early Hawaiians climbed to the volcano's edge to worship the gods.

About This Site   The top of Haleakala reaches over 10,000 feet above sea level, and the park encompasses 28,000 miles of land. Of this, 19,000 acres are wilderness that have been declared a biosphere reserve as of 1980. The windward slopes support a lush rainforest, and the Kipahulu section has an incredible chain of pools complete with cascades, herbs, and all manner of greenery. This region is among the best for hiking, while other parts of the park offer camping and bird watching.

One thing you cannot miss during your trip is the rare silverword plant. This blossoms once, then dies after yielding its beauty to the sun. The silverword is protected on these lands, having at one time numbered only 100 remaining plants. Also, watch the earth for sparkling stones. Green olivine and black augite dot cinder cones everywhere.

Activities   While Haleakala is beautiful by day, night is even more impressive, as this is one of the most accessible, high, open sky-watching regions. Go out and wish on a falling star. Count meteorites. An even number portends a great vacation!

If a mist appears at Haleakala, stand and watch to see if you can see your shadow in the halo effect. This is called "the Spectre of Brocken" and it's said to reveal your true soul. Look closely and know yourself as part of this sacredness.

No matter who your patron god/dess is, leave a small offering for him or her here as the ancients did. Whisper your name and wishes into the crater, to the sky, and the sun. Then continue to simply enjoy the tremendous beauty of this place with a thankful heart.

Side Trips   While you're on the island of Maui, it is well worth a day to go to Iao Valley, also known as the Valley of Kings. The ancient Hawaiians buried heroes here, likely because of its beauty. Even Mark Twain called this the Yosemite of the Pacific! There are areas in Iao that are so deep in the crater that they've never been touched by a sunrise or sunset. Rivers run throughout the valley, many of which have orchids and moonstones adorning them. You'll find Iao above Wailtuku town, readily accessible by auto.

Alternatively, go to the westernmost point of Maui to Black Rock. From this spot, spirits of the dead begin the journey to the next life or to the home of the ancestors.

HENGSHAN, CHINA
Elements: Air, earth
Themes: Meditation, herbalism, spirit communion, offering

There are actually two mountains named Hengshan in China, one to the south and one to the north. This particular mountain guardian is located in the central Hunyan district of China. It's about forty miles away from Datong, a mining city, which is one option for accommodations (but it's not an overly attractive area). Alternatively, look into staying in the village of nearby Hengshan, which has a reputation for marvelous teas, sweet pears, and mandarin oranges.

Consider planning your trip in the months of July through September during the annual fair that celebrates the local religious culture, arts, and sports. Or find out when the eighth month of the lunar year is currently, so you can watch the traditional pilgrimages.

For more information, look to any of these Web sites: www.cnta.com; www.china-window.com; www.great-china.net. Or, call the China National Tourist Office at 212-760-9700.

History and Folklore   The Hunyan region of China has a rich history, including being credited for producing the first fabric paper in the world. Here, this mountain stands like a watchtower as one of five sacred peaks in China, all of which are very important to Buddhists and Taoists alike. This is not surprising when you consider that the art of *feng shui* considered mountains a kind of guardian spirit that helps channel the earth's positive energy (*chi*).

In this part of the world (and many others) mountains also represent a bridge between the worlds. The tallest peaks are supportive towers holding up the four corners of creation, and some of them are said to be dwelling places for immortals whose knowledge of herbalism allows them to live to be hundreds of years old. To this day, this mountain and other peaks in China are favored by religious people as meditative sites where one can come to understand *tao* (the way of living in symmetry with the all things).

About This Site   Hengshan is considered one of the most important natural attractions in China. Local people say that once you've seen it, you never need to see another mountain again, which is easy to understand as you stand atop and can see for fifty miles around.

In the midst of the towering stone all around is a unique site—a monastery that hangs off the cliffs. Sometimes called the Flying Temple, its creators were called "feathered scholars" because of this unique creation. From the monastery through the mountains stretches a staircase going up to the summit (nearly 6,500 feet high).

Activities   Along the route upward you can stop at a bronze urn and give an offering of incense to whatever image of the divine seems suited to this moment. Traditionally, this particular spot outside the shrine of Lu Tung-pin (an immortal) also honors the god of agriculture, and it's a good place to give thanks for your blessings.

If you're a budding herbalist, any point on the mountain is a good place to pray and meditate for aid and inspiration in your art. The spirits of the immortals here can then begin to act as mentors and guides in your discovery of plant powers and properties.

Side Trip   Go to see the Dragon Palace in the Wulingyuan Tourist area, seventeen kilometers southwest of Guiyang. This amazing area is a mix of a subtropical forest with rock columns, natural botanical gardens, and a zoo. In the midst of this is a completely clear waterfall inside a deep cave adorned by stalactites and stalagmites.

KATAHDIN, MAINE
Elements: Earth, water, air
Themes: Bardic energy, protection, weather, invisibility

Mount Katahdin is the tallest of the Longfellow Mountains, located in Maine's north woods. For accommodations, I suggest staying in Lincoln, which has Interstate 95 running through it, and a nice scenic route (Route 2) that goes along the river. Lincoln is only thirty-four minutes from the airport and offers camping, thirteen lakes, swimming, frontier areas, water sports, winter activities, and very friendly residents. Mount Katahdin looms over the town in the northeastern background, as if to keep an eye on things!

For more information, contact the Lincoln Chamber of Commerce at 888-794-8065, the Maine Office of Tourism at 800-533-9595, Mount Katahdin Chamber of Commerce at 207-723-4443, or refer to www.visitmaine.com.

History and Folklore   Known as the spot where Henry David Thoreau climbed in the mid-1800s, local legends say that only daring people climb this mountain because the top is sacred to the Abenaki people, who believe it to be the home of a powerful spirit, Pomola. Pomola has the head of a moose, wings like an eagle, and a human body. From the peak of Katahdin, Pomola watches over weather and can be called on to help bring rain or storms.

It's estimated that the Abenaki have lived in this area for over 10,000 years. They're often referred to as "invisible people" because early histories briefly talk about the culture, then the Abenaki disappear from record, having been silenced by misunderstanding, sickness, and other situational difficulties. What we do know, however, is that storytelling is very important to this tribe as a way of teaching important lessons, including our connection to the land.

About This Site   Mount Katahdin marks the end of the 2,000-plus mile long Appalachian trail. It reaches to a height of 5,267 feet above sea level and challenges hikers with its difficult, rocky trails. Alongside the crags and cliffs, there are beautiful streams, one of which is named after Thoreau. Waterfalls also shimmer against stone escarpments. As you get into the higher parts of the mountainside, the temperature often drops and hiking trails become more treacherous, so be prepared.

Activities   Considering the Abenaki's love of good stories, and the fact that Thoreau found this area so inspiring, this is a perfect place to motivate your creative self. Take a sip of water from Thoreau's stream and internalize some of regional tenacity, wisdom, and creativity.

Afterward, sit quietly and think about well-loved magical stories: those from your tradition, those you've heard at the fireside, even those you remember from your childhood. Write these down in a journal to share with other like-minded people in the future. Better yet, write a story of your own—about creation, about why different types of weather happen, about ancestral spirits and archetypal powers. Let the spirits of the Abenaki, the Pomola, and Thoreau fill your pen and heart.

Also, if you're feeling overexposed in any situation, let the Abenaki ancestors teach you about invisibility. Meditate somewhere private, and as you do visualize yourself in that exact spot. Slowly, see the edges of your body fading into the trees, the grass, the water. Become one with your surroundings, and you will slowly fade from obvious view! When you master this technique, you can use it anywhere, anytime, to make yourself less noticeable.

KATARAGAMA, SRI LANKA
Element: Water
Themes: Vows and promises, recovering lost things, success, victory

Sri Lanka means "beautiful island," and beauty is something you can expect throughout your trip. While it is several hours drive away from Kataragama, your best bet for a wide variety of housing, food, shopping, and other amenities is Columbo, the former capital city (with an airport) under thirty minutes away. Columbo is located in western Sri Lanka, and it houses numerous temples, mosques, churches, a zoo, art galleries, and a museum. Here you can also experience the "devil dancing" of the Sinhalese up close, and the wonder of the sacred Bo-Tree where Buddha achieved enlightenment.

Tours of the city are readily available with a guide for about $20 for a car full of people. Consider traveling in July or August when Katharagama holds its annual festival, which celebrates the God's marriage to a Vedda princess. Travel between January and April if you're a bird lover and want to see a variety of migrating birds. For more information, refer to www.lanka.net, or call the tourism bureau at 94-01-4370599 or the embassy at 202-232-7181.

History and Folklore   Local legends claim that when the Bo-Tree arrived as a sapling in northern Indian some 2,500 years ago, the Kataragama warriors were present to pay homage and respect. But the Buddhists are not the only ones with stories to tell here. Kataragama is sacred to the Hindu war god Skanda, Muslims pray at a mosque here, and even Christians make journeys to the area.

No matter the religion, however, one theme appears again and again. People travel to this spot to try and find lost things or people, and to make promises. The promises are often accompanied with various piercings or fire walking, as if to give the gods a show of faith and true intention. At other times, people come simply to worship and leave offerings, then bless the region's supply of water.

About This Site   Today Kataragama is a township growing quickly in southern Sri Lanka. Located about two hundred kilometers away from Columbo, it was one of the sixteen places where Buddha visited in his spiritual pilgrimage.

Kataragama has a Hindu shrine and a Buddhist pagoda among other sites that you can wander to. In particular, take the time to see Waedahiti Kanda, which is just outside of the town. It is here that the Kataragama god lives, watching over the country and its people. All Sri Lankans revere this deity as a helper for overcoming problems and bringing business success.

Activities   If you wish to make a promise to someone (or a god/dess) or need to reclaim a lost item, stop at the temple or shrine of your choice and pour out a libation of water with your heart's desire. Or, if you're facing harsh difficulties or could use a little boost with your professional life, go to the base of Waedahiti Kanda instead, and pour your water there. Give the god his due so he may bless your efforts.

Side Trips Three possibilities come to mind. First is Sigiriya, one of Sri Lanka's most important archaeological sites, having been a royal citadel for nearly twenty years. Sigiriya is preceded by a huge pathway of red rock, some of which is so highly polished that you can see your reflection in the rain. The name *Sigiriya* means "lion's throat," which describes the carving through which all travelers had to pass—now all that remains are part of the lion's paws.

Second is Damubulla, twelve miles away from Sigiriya. This rock mass houses a temple dating to the first century B.C. From the top of this area you can see for miles around, and the five caves nearby have become shrines. The first includes a 47-foot-long image of the Buddha (hand-carved), and the third has 150 different statues of the gods.

Finally is Sri Pada, the holy mountain near Kandy where the Buddha was thought to have first stepped foot on earth. Near the peak of the mountain, a boulder bears a footprint. People make pilgrimages here at dawn to improve their chances of finding the same enlightenment as the great teacher.

KATHMANDU VALLEY, NEPAL
Element: Spirit
Themes: Courage, banishing, prayer, enlightenment, friendship

Kathmandu is located in the Middle Basin of Nepal. It has an international airport, making it readily accessible to travelers. The city is a thriving area where you'll find plentiful hotels, transportation, food, and sites. It's also a backpacker's paradise.

But, as the old saying goes, "Don't drink the water." Carry bottled water with you everywhere as a precaution.

Tourist season is October–December (after monsoon season), when the Deshain and Tihar festivals take place with a flavor similar to Christmas in the states. It is suggested you pre-book your reservations, though many accommodations can be found at the last minute. But don't expect late night revelry. Most attractions in Kathmandu close early, due to the local rising hour of 4 A.M.!

Specific tourist information is available through the Nepal Embassy at 202-667-4550, or on-line at www.info-nepal.com.

History and Folklore   Kathmandu has a unique charm, pageantry, and spirit all its own. The pace of life speaks of a time long forgotten, with values and ideas that were simpler. This is especially true because the country wasn't open to outsiders for 150 years. So, don't expect anything in Nepal to be timely or fast paced—pack your patience with your clothes.

The city was founded in A.D. 723 at the crossroads of two trade routes, one to India and one to China. This made for an amazing mingling of peoples and ideologies, not to mention an exchange of information.

The strong Hindu and Buddhist influence, mannerisms, and traditions throughout the region are unmistakable, and will definitely impact your trip. For example, always use your right hand when passing food or while eating; the left hand is considered tainted. Don't take pictures of any temples or try to enter without permission, as outsiders aren't always allowed or welcome. Lightweight pants are recommended for both men and women as being appropriate garb, and keep public displays of affection to a minimum.

About This Site   Kathmandu is the cultural heart of Nepal. While there are certainly many rose-brick temples to visit, the locals will be happy to suggest seeing the shopping area where you can haggle 'til you drop. Durbar Square is an earthy site — one of the best to gather fresh greens and to view the natives worshiping at statues covered in garlands and other small offerings. The streets are difficult to navigate, being very narrow, but almost everyone will happily help with directions should you lose your way.

There is an amazing Healing Center in the center of the city that teaches ancient techniques, from Thai massage to Shiatsu and Yoga. Another interesting site is the Kasthamandap building built around the twelfth century, which houses a community center. Adjacent to this you'll find a temple to Shiva overlooking salespeople and tourists alike. Beyond this, there are numerous other sacred places in the valley, including Lake Taudaha, the home of the god Karkaroka, and Kumari Chowk, the home of the living goddess.

Activities   Go to the great bell and wait for it to be rung. This will ward off any evil spirits who threaten your happiness or the safety of your travels. Or, if you feel the need to add some spice to your love life, stop by the Jaganath Temple, which houses a huge display of erotic carvings.

Another good venture is stopping by Hanuman Dhoka, the old royal palace adjacent to Durbar Square. Within you'll find a statue that commemorates the monkey god's assistance to Rama. Pray here to receive courage for any difficulty facing you.

Next, stop at the friendship bridge between Nepal and Kathmandu. Think fondly of a friend here and pray for blessings on that person. Finally, just for fun go to the area called Freak Street (Jochne). Here you'll find prayer wheels, incense, and all the tools you could ever want in your quest for enlightenment.

Side Trips   Helambu (seventy kilometers northeast) has wonderful scenery and several Buddhist monasteries and Pokhara Valley (two hundred kilometers west) is tremendously lovely, complete with three lakes that are fed from glacial waters in the Himalayas.

KEITH BRIDGE PARK, GAINESVILLE, GEORGIA
Elements: Water, earth
Themes: Stability, peace

This magickal place is located in the foothills of the Georgia
Blue Ridge Mountains of Forsythe County, on Lake Lanier, five
miles west of the Georgia 400—a major highway that experiences traffic jams during peak rush hours and some weekends.
Lodging is most reasonable in Gainesville, but also available at
the Lake Lanier Islands complex. Keith Bridge Park offers plentiful parking.

In terms of timing your trip, consider going in April when
the dogwood trees blossom and the weather is still comfortable
for people accustomed to cooler climes. For more information,
call the Georgia Tourism Department at 800-847-4842.

History and Folklore Lake Lanier was named after
Sidney Clopton Lanier, who wrote the "Song of the Chatta-
hoochee," which describes this region's beauty. It is a man-made
lake that was developed to act as a resort region within driving
distance of Atlanta. Most recently, Lake Lanier hosted the 1996
Olympic Rowing, Canoe, and Kayak events.

About This Site Located in the heart of Cherokee country,
Keith Bridge Park is fairly small (you can traverse it in about
forty-five minutes by foot). Being adjacent to Lake Sidney Lanier,
with over five hundred miles of shoreline to enjoy, Keith Bridge
Park has beaches, playgrounds, and picnic areas with pavilions
for gatherings, if desired. The beaches have lifeguards on duty.

The Lake Lanier Islands are also nearby—if you don't mind
a lot of tourists. This complex offers theme parks, tennis, golf,
boating, and additional picnic sites. For on-line tourist information and maps, refer to www.lakelanier.com/welcome.htm.

Activities The lake creates a mixture of water and earth
energies that really allows a person to relax. Try sitting on some

of the rocks near the parking lot (bring ear plugs to tune out distractions) and looking out upon the water. These rocks are perfectly suited to thoughtful meditation and daydreaming.

A quarter mile from the parking lot, off a trail, is a small peninsula with trees, crystals, marble, and other beautiful earthy trinkets to use in creating sacred space or for meditative purposes. This is surrounded by large rocks and water, so you can dangle your feet and enjoy the mingling elements firsthand (or foot, as the case may be).

Walk along the beach in an attitude of prayer. Watch for a gift from the water (like a shell). Pick this up and meditate with it to hear the voices of earth and lake singing together. Keep this with you as a charm to draw serenity into your life.

At sunset, when the solar sphere touches the water, consider enjoying the mixture of fire-water-earth to energize and center your spirit. Visualize the sun's colors pouring toward you over the waters, into your soul. Or do a spell for stability while sitting on one of the ancient stones.

KNOSSOS PALACE, CRETE
Elements: Earth, water
Themes: Earth magic, fertility, rejuvenation

Crete is the largest island in Greece, readily accessible by ferry from Piraeus, or airplane from Athens, Mykonos, and Thessaloniki. It offers a wide variety of art, architecture, and recreation to please nearly any traveler's desires and pocketbook. Food on the island is delicious, especially the cheese and wine. There are hotels in Knossos, complete with spas, that will make your stay pleasant and physically rejuvenating.

There are also several towns that you can visit to fill out your stay. The town of Siteia offers archaeological and folk museums, and Zakros village has an amazing palm forest and beautiful beaches. In terms of travel time, consider going in spring (March 1) to see the Procession of the Swallows, which welcomes this season of hope and renewal. The songs of this ritual are over 2,000 years old, and the rite itself is said to encourage fertility and health in both animals and people.

For more information, contact the Greek National Tourist Organization at 212-421-5777. Or, if you're looking for a tour group to go with, check into Power Places Tours (800-234-8687). This group offers regular vacations to different sacred sites, complete with airfare, lodging, and spiritual leaders to guide your experience.

History and Folklore The ancient Phoenicians and Minoans created a beautiful civilization here that was filled with abundant magic. The island proved fertile for olive and grapes, perfect for making oil and wine to trade throughout the Aegean region. Alongside this rich civilization, the Greek myths and lore thrived.

It was common for the people of Crete to simply stand by the sea or on a high cliff to worship the Earth Mother, Rhea, who is said to live in Mount Ida. It was also a common custom to build resplendent buildings like Knossos, as the home for kings. The Palace of Knossos was built around 2,000 B.C., complete with labyrinths, bronze goddess figurines, and murals depicting Tauropolis, the fertile bull goddess. This palace became the center of Minoan life, from the arts to government and trade.

About This Site Considered among the most powerful sacred sites for accessing the goddess and her ancient energies, the palace of Knossos features a portrait of the earth goddess with three faces, representing the maiden, mother, and crone. It also has an incredible dolphin fresco, symbolizing our ancient ties to the water and all creation. With this said, it would be difficult to miss the influence of the water element here since the island air is filled with salty-sea aromas. Water is also feminine, healing, and nurturing, accenting the goddess's well-grounded energy with inspiration, fruitfulness, and healing.

If you find yourself overwhelmed with the feminine energies here, you can go to Mount Ida to the caves and leave an offering for Zeus. This craggy cave, filled with oddly shaped features (some of which are very phallic) is said to be the place of his birth, thanks to the myth of Zeus's mother hiding him here. The cave isn't terribly far from the palace.

Activities   While the exterior of the building has experienced decay over the years, the glory of what once was still reverberates here, singing the song of the Mother. Sit on the ground near the palace, breathe deeply, and listen. Hear your heartbeat pounding with the same rhythm of the earth below you. Hear how the two blend together into harmony and allow your soul and body to be refreshed.

If you or someone you know wishes to conceive a child, gather up a little soil from this region, and ask both Rhea and Tauropolis to infuse it with fertile energies.

Side Trip   If you're staying in this area for a week or so, go into Athens and see the ancient temple at Delphi. Here you can access the ancient insightful powers of divination (don't forget to bring your favorite divination tool to charge it up)! Or, if you like, learn a whole new system of divination. The Greeks favored interpreting the movement of birds, the meaning of found feathers, and lot-casting with beans.

While in Athens, you can also take in the Parthenon, dedicated to the goddess of wisdom, Athena; the temple of Zeus; and the Acropolis for a true taste of local culture and the magnificence of Greek myths.

L'ANSE AMOUR, LABRADOR
Elements: Water, earth
Themes: Death, offering, supplication

L'Anse Amour is located on the Labrador Straits. You can reach it by ferry or by car along Route 510. Here you'll be visiting a historical Indian burial site. The timing of your trip is purely personal, but spring is probably the nicest, weather-wise. Alternatively, by coming during summer you'll be able to go whale-watching off the Strait of Belle Isle. Quite a variety move through this region including potheads, killer whales, humpbacks, fins, and also several types of porpoises and dolphins.

For more information, you can call 800-563-6353 to receive a free brochure, or check out these Web sites: www. govinf.ca/tourism and www.wordplay.com/tourism/labrador.

History and Folklore   The people of Labrador are descendants of the Thule Inuit, who came here from Greenland, and the Dorset Eskimos, who have lived on the coast for 2,000 years. As a group, they were predominantly hunters and traders. Even before this, however, Labrador was the home of aboriginal people who lived on the edge of glaciers, and whose burial remains dot the area as a silent memorial to primitive beliefs.

About This Site   Labrador is very rough country, filled with steep mountains, barren rock, and lonely valleys. The predominant element by far is water, embodied by lakes, the ocean, rivers, and snow. To this base, a bit of earth gets mingled in through the wildlife and spruce trees, which were once vital for fuel, shelter, and transportation (e.g., kayaks).

The site itself is the oldest known aboriginal burial mound in North America, dating back 7,500 years. This site houses the remains of a young boy, wrapped in a bark shroud, lying east to west, with a walrus tusk, harpoon head, and bone whistle nearby. Around him fires were lit and offerings made, then the mound was constructed over the top afterward.

No one knows this child's name or his social status. What we do know is that this was probably more than an attempt at aiding the spirit's passage into its next existence. It may, in fact, have been a way of petitioning the gods for help during a particularly difficult year.

Activities   As a rather odd contrast to this ancientness, just outside L'Anse Amour there's a beautiful lighthouse built in the 1850s—a perfect setting for a romantic evening, stargazing, collecting water-energized gifts from the sea, or taking long meditative walks. By climbing the house's 122 steps, you'll enjoy a view that's impossible to forget. Along the beach, you'll find starfish, mussels, and other items dotting the shore, perfect for gathering and using in the western point of your sacred space or as a representation of the water element on your altar.

Side Trips   See the Bishop's Mitre, a mountain near Labrador City. This lovely peak is thought to be the abode of an ancient Native American deity. Many people buried in this region were uncovered, bearing amulets with the mountain's symbol. These tokens acted as a kind of protection in the afterlife (and perhaps also for the body to keep it safe from predators).

Or go to Fire Lake, which is an hour and three-quarters drive from Gagnon. This lake is a neat blend of fire and water, because the horizon sometimes seems to glow at sunset, and thus comes the name!

LOOKOUT MOUNTAIN, TENNESSEE
Elements: Earth, water, air
Themes: Love, relationships, devotion, vows

Lookout Mountain is located about two hours from Atlanta or Nashville and three hours from the Smoky Mountains, off I-24. For this adventure you'll probably want to find accommodations in Chattanooga, which is nestled in the Tennessee Mountains and has ready access to your destination. There are hotel and motel accommodations, numerous eateries, a nature center, and a reflection garden (423-821-1160) in Chattanooga, along with tour operators and tourist services.

If you can travel during the first week of October, spend some time in Jonesborough for the National Storytelling Festival. This event preserves the bardic traditions and is highlighted with sacred stories, ghost tales, myths, and legends to tickle the magical heart and spirit. For more information about this event, call 800-525-4514.

For general regional information on-line, refer to: www.chattanooga.gov/index or www.chattanooga.net/cvb. You can also call the Chattanooga Convention and Visitors Bureau at 800-231-4636, or the Department of Tourist Development at 615-741-2158 (www.state.tn.us).

History and Folklore   Lookout Mountain's history begins around 200 million years ago. An ancient sea bed became the depository for bits of limestone, shale, and sand. Slowly, each layer hardened and then was pushed upward by a series of earthquakes. While the mountain raised its head from the waters, some of it cracked, forming joints along which places like Ruby Falls (see "About This Site") and Lookout Caverns formed.

Native Americans used the base of the mountain as a campsite, and the rugged countryside often provided a hiding place for vagabonds and outlaws. The caverns were discovered in 1928 by a landowner, who named the falls after his beloved wife, Ruby. This makes the falls a favorite site for honeymooners.

About This Site   Lookout Mountain is known for unusual geological features, especially Ruby Falls, an underground waterfall, and Lookout Caverns, two caves with deposits of various minerals from water seepage on the walls, floor, and ceiling. These deposits form a wonderful variety of columns, drapes, flowstone, and stalactites. Some of the groupings have names such as the Hall of Dreams, with its mystical helicites, and the Onyx Jungle, with towering pillars for trees.

Ruby Falls forms at the end of one of the Lookout Caves, dropping 145 feet into a pool that eventually flows out into the Tennessee River. The falls are generally open 8 A.M.– 8 P.M., and the most recently posted entry fee was $9.00 for adults, $4.50 for children. More information about this particular site can be obtained by calling 423-821-2544

Activities   Go to Lover's Leap, a high point on Lookout Mountain. Many people consider this spot a power point that seems to hold "good vibrations"—a kind of warmth that one would not expect from a simple outcropping of stones touching the sky and air. From here, you can see no less than seven states. Magically speaking, seven is the number of completion and fulfillment, so this is a perfect spot for making vows and casting spells aimed at improving relationships in general. Whisper your desires to the winds and let them carry that prayer across the land as far as your eyes can see and beyond. Scatter rose petals here to spread love around the country, then gather up a pebble to carry self-love home with you. The possibilities are as endless as your imagination will allow.

Alternatively, make a wish when you see Ruby Falls. Dip a small rose quartz crystal in the waters to energize it, and rededicate yourself to love's quest. Be it love of a job, a friend, a project, or a life-mate, love's power can transform every corner of your life with a little magic for motivation.

Side Trips   Just over the border in Georgia you can enjoy Cloudland Canyon. Originally, Cloudland Canyon was part of an ancient oceanside beach. Thanks to erosion and shifting earth, it now appears like a huge tear, dropping over 1,000 feet from the rim to the floor. It is part of a park that includes campsites, cottages, picnic sites, tennis, swimming, hiking, and many other activities for tourists.

Cloudland Canyon is noted for having a high level of spirit activity and energy. Communing with nature spirits or communicating with one's spirit guides is not difficult here as long as you have some privacy. You can get directions and more information by calling 706-657-4050.

MACHU PICCHU, PERU
Element: Fire
Themes: Sun magic, knot magic

Cuzco is a good choice for lodging. As the oldest continually inhabited city in South America, Cuzco hosts all manner of Incan dancing, music, prayers, and costumes, performed by descendants of these ancient magical people. Here you'll find highly adorned buildings touched with gold and silver, known respectively as "the sweat of the sun" and "tears of the moon." Tour buses are readily available from the city to Machu Picchu, and trains come through the area daily.

You'll find a variety of food and dry goods available to you throughout Peru. The best months for travel are June to September, when the mountains aren't wet. If possible, visit during June for the solstice. Among the Incas, this was a holy time that marked the sun's rebirth.

Be aware that this area is very politically sensitive, often becoming a hot spot for terrorism. Check with travel agents before planning a vacation, or call the Peruvian Embassy at 202-833-9860

History and Folklore   Machu Picchu is called the Lost City of the Incas, built over 2,000 years ago and located in a mountain at the heart of a rainforest. Here the natives enriched both mind and spirit, never separating everyday life from their beliefs. The full purpose of the city has been lost to antiquity, but it was likely a ceremonial site and place for public gatherings.

The Incas considered themselves children of the sun and their culture was steeped heavily in shamanism and witchcraft. Remnants of this can still be found on many street corners where native vendors offer love potions, power pouches, and magical knots for protection and safe journeys. Local mythology says that the ancient gods still live in the mountains around the region, and in modern times numerous UFO sightings have been reported locally.

About This Site   Nestled near Urubama, the sacred valley of the Incas, Machu Picchu is the perfect locale in which to nurture your soul and inspire your spirit. It's built into a mountain so that it mingles with the stone, and the surrounding cliffs watch over you like sentinels.

Visitors to this area say that pictures don't do it justice. The ruins, which once acted as the nucleus for a twelve-million-person empire, sit at 8,000 feet atop a mountain looking straight down into two valleys. The stone road rambles out of the area, staying close to the mountain and leading to the Gate of the Sun going toward Cuzco. The best word to describe the panorama is breathtaking.

Activities   Go to the Temple of the Sun at sunrise and greet the ancient fire gods. Reach your hands out to the horizon with a long strand of rope and begin tying ten knots into it. This binds the sun energy inside so you can open it for warmth and energy in the future as needed.

If you need lunar energy instead, wait for moonrise and follow the same procedure. The Incas believed in the moon's power almost as strongly as the sun's. In this case, however, untie a knot when you need to empower a spell, improve personal psychism, or to encourage a visionary dream.

Also, consider taking a walk along the Inca trail, which begins in Cuzco and leads to Macchu Picchu through mountains and valleys. It takes four or five days to traverse by foot, but you'll get a much better feel for the sacredness of the region this way. If you decide to try this, take plenty of coca leaves and tea with you to cure altitude sickness.

Side Trip   Treat yourself to an aerial view of the Nazka lines, which crisscross the southern desert with patterns whose meanings are still being studied. Some of the images marked the Wheel of the Year, others marked pathways that one would walk to sacred places. Others still remain a mystery. The cost of an air tour is about $50–$60, but that usually includes a side trip to the necropolis.

MAMMOTH CAVE, KENTUCKY
Elements: Earth, water
Themes: Creativity, beauty

Mammoth Cave is located in south-central Kentucky, easily accessed by Interstate 65 south of Louisville. It's about twenty-eight miles from Bowling Green, but look for lodging (including bed-and-breakfast facilities), campsites, restaurants, and tourist information in Cave City, off Route 1. To call ahead for information on Mammoth Park, dial 502-758-2328, the National Parks Service. Or you can call the Kentucky Department of Travel at 800-225-8747. On-line information is available at www.tourky.com/tourky/html.

In terms of travel time, if you're a horse lover you might like to venture out to arrive around the first Saturday of May and take in the Kentucky Derby in Louisville before heading south.

History and Folklore   The caves were first discovered in the late 1700s, but were probably used by Native Americans long before that. Mammoth Cave yielded numerous raw ingredients, specifically saltpeter, which was used in the making of gunpowder and epsom salts. During the early 1800s the region slowly developed into a tourist site, due to the extraordinary cave features.

About This Site   These caves were formed out of lime-stone, thanks to underground water flows, and are part of over 8,000 miles of caverns in this region. The temperature in the cave averages around 50 degrees, the upper galleries being dry and the lower ones damp from various pools and rivers.

There are numerous beautiful sites inside Mammoth Cave, ranging from stalactites and stalagmites to sightless fish. One impressive area is Echo River, which has a 200-foot vaulted ceil-ing draped with calcite. This unique feature allows the stones here to resonate for up to thirty seconds with specific sounds, echoing the song of earth and water mingling together. Other majestic areas include: the Pillars of Hercules, a huge set of columns; the Bridal Altar, a functional shrine where many people get married; and the Star Chamber, which is dark but for the magnesium sulphate stone that glows overhead.

Activities   The mingling of water and earth here makes it a perfect spot to empower any creative project that you might be considering. The water inspires while the earth gives you a strong substructure to build on, so that your efforts are long-lasting. Perhaps you could gather up a stone from the caves (if permitted) and keep it next to your effort. Or carry the token with you to give your dreams good foundations to grow in.

If you need a boost of self-confidence, meditate outside the caves for a while. Think about how simple and unassuming the cave looks—even perhaps frightening from the outside. Yet once within, it is altogether lovely. This is a powerful truth to inter-nalize about people, too. Externals mean very little—don't worry so much about the packaging but consider it a window of what you're building within.

Side Trips   Mammoth Cave is located near several other caves you might wish to visit while you're here. Onyx Cave has very well-preserved formations, Diamond Caverns' crystal for-mations will keep any Wiccan amused for hours, and Kentucky Caverns have incredibly colored stalactites and stalagmites.

MANITOULIN ISLAND, ONTARIO, CANADA
Elements: Water, earth
Themes: Creativity, ancestral and land spirits, dreams

Manitoulin Island is in the heart of Rainbow Country, accessible by Highway 6, or by the Chi-Chee-Maun Ferry from Tobermory, Ontario. Some lodging is available on the island itself. The Township of Howland (705-368-2009) is one good choice for accommodations, as it is very involved in the local tourist industry. Howland offers parks, snowmobile trails, hiking, a marina, camping facilities, museums, and archaeological sites to fill your free time.

For more information, contact the Manitoulin Tourism Association at 705-368-3021 (summer), 705-368-3021 (winter), or at www.georgianbay.com/sites.

History and Folklore   Being the home of the Ojibway Indians (whose legends helped give birth to the "Song of Hiawatha"), Manitoulin and the entire Lake Superior area have many bits of folklore associated with them. The name *Manitoulin* says much in itself: it means "power of the Manitous," which is a type of regional spirit.

The Ojibway people believe that the island lies along a route that will lead them to the sacred Thunderbird, a potent god whose wings beat out thunder, and whose eyes flash with lightning. Why venerate such a being? Because along with the thunder and lightning, Thunderbird bears nourishing rains for the crops.

About This Site   Manitoulin is the largest island in the world surrounded by fresh water. Of particular interest here is Dreamer's Rock, whose power is said to inspire many things: flashbacks to past lives, communications from ancestors, and psychic dreams, just to name a few (see "Activities").

Upon arrival, you can expect the sights, sounds, and smells of any marine-rich area. The docks reach out to greet boats of various sizes, people line the shores, lazily fishing, and small shops dot the area, including the Tourist's Association office located near the swing bridge at Little Current. The overall feeling here is one of relaxation and welcome.

Around the island you may periodically run across rock art of the Ojibway people that honors the spirits of the land. According to tradition, these spirits come out to play tricks on unsuspecting folks. To appease them, simply leave an offering of tobacco or rum.

Activities Meditate at Dreamer's Rock (located on the Birch Island Reserve) to motivate your inventive spirit. This bit of land is believed to be pre-created and thus holds the life force within it. Young people originally came here to fast, pray, receive visions, and discover guardian spirits. Today, this spot draws people seeking purpose and focus, especially in the creative arts.

While you're here, consider reciting this beautiful traditional prayer from the Ojibway Indians, which reminds us of our need to reconnect with the land and each other:

"Grandfather, look at our brokenness. We know that in all creation only the human family has strayed from the Sacred Way. We know that we are the ones who are divided, and we are the ones who must come back together and walk in the Sacred Way. Grandfather, Sacred One, teach us love, compassion, and honor that we may heal the earth and heal each other."

Finally, gather up a pinch of dirt from the land (remember to say thank you to the spirits) and take it home. Put this under your pillow saying, "Dream, and remember what you dream." This was the command of Ojibway mothers to their children, because this tribe honors dreams as a treasured source of wisdom.

MECCA, SAUDI ARABIA
Elements: Water, earth
Themes: Pilgrimages, cleansing, communion, blessing

You will need a visa to enter Saudi Arabia, which can be obtained through the embassy at 202-342-3800 (337-4076 for general information). You can also contact the Cultural Office at 202-337-9450.

The best place to stay for sightseeing in Mecca or Medina is in the city of Jeddah. Jeddah is the second largest city in Saudi Arabia, sitting like a jewel on the Red Sea. Traditionally, pilgrims going on their *hajj* (pilgrimage) arrive in the port here, but it offers much to any traveler. Jeddah has an amusement park, leisure facilities, sailing, snorkeling, and amazing markets.

History and Folklore   Your host city has an old Arabic story associated with it. It says that when Adam and Eve were cast out of Paradise, Adam landed in Sri Lanka, and Eve landed near the port of Jeddah! Finally, the two met again at Mount Arafat, near Mecca. Upon arrival, Adam prayed that a shrine would be erected here, and his prayers were heard. Gabriel came with the magic stone for the shrine and ever since this has been the site of Abrahamic pilgrimages.

The Koran tells us that it is the sacred duty of all Muslims to go to Mecca once in a lifetime. Part of this tradition has to do with the well of Zamzam and the neighboring Ka'ba shrine, said to have been reconstructed by Abraham and Ishmael. The Ka'ba is rather unique, in that Israelite tradition says the black stone used in its construction was "sent down" to Abraham, alluding to a meteorite. This is very close to the Arabic story about Gabriel.

Another interesting yet often overlooked bit of history is that up until the seventh century A.D., the Ka'ba attracted followers from many walks of life because Arabians worshiped many gods and demi-gods. Islam changed that, but the diversity remains beneath as a legacy. To this day Mecca is considered a center of faith.

About This Site   The Ka'ba shrine is a huge hollow stone covered in gold-embroidered black cloth. Around it, a sea of people wearing white can often be seen—these are the pilgrims who have come here to fulfill one of the five pillars of Islam. Before arriving here they have paid debts and righted any wrongs so they might be acceptable—a testament to the sacredness of this spot.

Beyond the structure, the ancient 7-inch diameter stone, consisting of seven smaller stones, is mounted in silver. The east–west façades are aligned to greet the sunrise of summer solstice, and the south facade is directed to the rising of Canopus, a bright star. Tour guides will tell you that the stone was once white, but it turned black from all the kisses of sinful people who leave their evil behind here.

Activities   The most traditional activity is to go to Mecca as part of a pilgrimage. For women, this is difficult because you must be accompanied by a father, brother, or husband who helps with various parts of the pilgrim's rituals. Be that as it may, you'll find that at least 50 percent of all people undertaking this pilgrimage are women.

Before arriving in Mecca, wash yourself and don white clothing as a symbol of purification. Drink at the Zamzam, gathering a little water to take home for continued blessings, and pray at Arafat until sunset (this is where Mohammed preached his last sermon). The next day, toss seven stones at Eid-ul-Adha to throw away all evil. Then, finally, circle the Ka'ba, the black holy stone, to complete your spiritual journey.

While on the surface all of this may seem foreign to the Wiccan, seven *is* the magical number of completion, and we work our magic within the sacred circle. So by following the traditional route of the *hajj*, we follow our own sacred circle to cleanse negativity and return home refreshed.

Side Trips   About two hundred miles northeast of Mecca you can enjoy Medina, called the City of the Prophet. This was the earliest base for the Muslim faith and is considered second only to Mecca in its sacredness throughout the region.

MONTE ALBAN CEREMONIAL SITE, MEXICO
Element: Spirit
Themes: Ritual work, universal awareness

Monte Alban rises above the city of Oaxaca in southwest Mexico, being within a fifteen-minute drive along the Oaxaca-Monte Alban highway. The entire area is a tropical zone where you can anticipate hot, dry weather on the coast and hot, wet weather inland. You'll need to pace your visit according to the heat and your tolerance to it.

Oaxaca offers bed-and-breakfast facilities, hotels, tours, car and bike rentals, and resorts. Come prepared with some cash, however, as smaller establishments won't accept credit cards. You can reach the state tourism office at 011-951-4-7733, and they have an excellent on-line site at: www.mexiconline.com.

History and Folklore   The ruins of Monte Alban represent one of the largest ritual sites in ancient Mesoamerica. The first buildings were likely created around 800 B.C., with the majority having been constructed between A.D. 300 and 900. The stone was quarried from the valley nearby, which was no small feat for people who had little in the way of good tools and who had not yet discovered the wheel!

Monte Alban became a key ceremonial center and fortress in the region for the Olmeca, Mixteca, and Zapoteca cultures. Even so, it is very hard to understand why the people built such an important and complex site here, considering the lack of water and neighboring towns. Students of sacred geometry tell us the reason is that several ley lines intersect nearby, creating the perfect atmosphere for a temple.

About This Site Monte Alban is an amazing piece of architecture, complete with pyramids, tombs, and an astronomical observatory located on Mound J, which is aligned with the Southern Cross and Alpha Centauri. The remains look rather eerie against the sandy, flat backdrop with several stones laying around outside the main edifice. Even with the obvious decay, the energy here seems strong, sure, and enduring.

Some of the notable structures to look for include the Edifice of the Dancers, so named for its wall carvings, featuring people in various odd postures. The Ball Court was an actual playing arena, obvious by its rectangular base, slanted walls, and grasshopper sculpture nearby. There is also a great plaza with dozens of rooms to explore.

Activity As a ceremonial site for well over ten centuries, Monte Alban is an ideal location to consider the role that rituals and ceremonies have (or should have) in your life. In Wicca, ritual is a way of maintaining an awareness of earth's cycles, creating and directing energy, and communing with sacred powers. And while modern realities don't always allow for elaborate festivals, life itself can become our ritual and an act of worship if we allow it to be.

Besides this, spend a little time on Mound J contemplating how even the ancients looked to the heavens with hopefulness. Here they watched for signs and omens. Here they sought out answers to the universe's mysteries. And now you join them!

Side Trip While staying in Oaxaca, make sure you take in some of the area's more than two dozen temples and shrines. For example, Mitla became a major religious center after Monte Alban's downfall. Santo Domingo is an amazing sample of

Baroque architecture, as is the Basilica of our Lady of Solitude. These places, and others like them, mirror a local attitude that says miracles are a part of our everyday life—if we but watch for them!

Alternatively, Teotihuacan, the ancient part of Mexico City, is well worth the venture. Here there are amazing religious structures dating to 200 B.C. that honor the sun, the moon, the ancestors, and the creation of earth. The symbols here are impossible for any spiritual seeker to miss—pyramids, holy caves, clover-shaped floors (the four quarters of creation), and streets aligned with star groupings.

NARSAQ, GREENLAND
Elements: Fire, air
Themes: Sun and light magic, joy, luck, wishes

The easiest route into Narsaq is via Denmark or Iceland to the Narsarsuaq Airport. From here, you can take either a brief helicopter or ferry ride to Narsaq Town. While this is a tiny municipality, it offers hostels and bed-and-breakfast facilities for travelers and an abundance of hospitality. It's centrally located near numerous sites of interest, glacial tours run regularly from the docks, there's folk dancing for groups, and you will even have the chance to sing with the Greenland Choir!

For more information, contact the Denmark Tourist Bureau at 212-949-2333 or refer to www.greenland-gl.

History and Folklore   Narsaq has a very long history, with human inhabitants arriving here in 2000 B.C. The region has strong undertones of both the Inuit and Viking heritage because of its gentle climate and good hunting. Many people here can trace their family lines back to settlements established by Erik the Red (dating between A.D. 986 and 1500) or the Inuit of the Thule culture who settled in the mid-1300s.

One of the largest Viking settlements was originally situated in Narsaq, so ruins are found all around the area (see "About This Site"). In addition, a unique geological phenomena, a volcanic intrusion, allows for rare stones and minerals to be formed here, including Tugtupit and sodalite. You might focus on this particular feature of the area for more fiery energy.

About This Site   Considered part of the "midnight sun" region, life in Greenland has a suitably timeless appeal. People are used to doing "daytime" activities in total darkness, so one single day (or night) seems figuratively to never end.

From Narsaq you have a beautiful view of a neighboring mountain, fjords, and ice caps. But what you've come to see are the Viking ruins, the oldest of which go back to A.D. 985. Here, you can appreciate the Viking tenacity—they were very slow to adopt Christianity, seeing little benefit to it—so much is the case that Erik the Red and his wife didn't live together after her conversion!

Not terribly far from here in Qassiarsuk is Erik the Red's residence. Both regions have Inuit sites, too, which makes for an interesting study in cultural variety!

Activities   If you travel in winter, spend as much time as possible outdoors sky gazing. If your timing is good, you'll catch a glimpse of the Northern Lights. To see them brings good luck and happiness, as folklore tells us these are actually ancestral spirits dancing for joy! You might want to whisper a wish to them and let the frosty winds carry it across the land and to the heavens. Also, make a mental note of what color the lights are when you see them: you can use this color of light again any time you need to re-stimulate happiness and good fortune in your life (use a colored light bulb for this).

If you travel between May 25 and July 25, this is when the sun never sets. It's the perfect opportunity to enact any solar-related spells and rituals, and generally some serious sun worship (not the tanning kind, either).

Finally, if you can find or buy a Tugtupit stone, hold it in your hand or expose it to sunlight. What once seemed to be a pale red stone is actually a vibrant red gem that will bring you luck.

Side Trips   If you have some extra time to spend in Denmark, there's an interesting site on the northern border. In Lindholm Hoje you'll find an ancient Viking necropolis, complete with boat-shaped burial grounds to carry the heroic souls safely to the afterlife in Valhalla.

NATURAL ARCHES, BERMUDA
Elements: Water, earth
Themes: Transformation, victory, luck

Truthfully, all of Bermuda is so beautiful that it could easily be considered a power center unto itself. Located in the northwestern Atlantic, this is one of the oldest dependent territories of Great Britain. There are three good Web sites dedicated to Bermuda travel: bermuda.com, bermudatourism.org, and bermuda-online.com., or call 800-223-6016.

For this particular journey you'll want to arrange for a guest cottage in Tucker's Town. These houses line the coral pink beaches, provide privacy and are all highly accessible to the rest of the island; the natural arches are right here on the beachfront. Reservations and information are available at info@pinkbeach.com or by calling 800-355-6161.

In terms of travel times, consider going in late April if you're planning a side trip into St. George (see later in this section). You'll get to enjoy the peppercorn ceremony, complete with parades and costumes, to commemorate the collection of rent: a peppercorn. According to tradition, this custom must continue for the region to thrive.

History and Folklore   Bermuda was discovered in the 1500s. The islands were formed of limestone and coral, and the lush greenery has inspired numerous great minds, including Mark Twain, who described it as having "breezy groves . . . and lovely vistas of blue water."

In magical history, Bermuda holds a dubious distinction. The colonial city of St. George, founded in 1612, hosted witch trials and executions earlier than those held in Salem, Massachusetts. St. George is only fifteen minutes away from the recommended cottages, and it's a good place to visit if you wish to help put the spirits of some Cunning Folk to rest and honor the lives needlessly lost there.

About This Site   A feast of flowers is what comes immediately to mind. The people of Bermuda are avid gardeners, and this shows. No matter where you go, you'll see gardens that rival, if not surpass, those of Victorian England and America. Butterflies tend to be abundant because of this, which makes an incredible view when they all take flight at once! I dare you to feel anything but happy at that moment.

The Natural Arches are a wonder to behold, especially at sunrise or sunset. It looks as if mother nature opened a doorway and is inviting you to step through into another place and time. When the surf gets a little more active, the splashing of water with sunlight makes for an energetic dance you'll never forget.

Activities   Metaphysically, archways represent a meeting place between the worlds, in addition to change and victory. By passing beneath an arch, you can leave the old behind and emerge reborn in spirit. For this purpose you can go to the archways just before sunrise. Wait on one side in the dark, draining yourself of any residual negativity, unwanted habits, and outmoded ideals. Then as the first hint of sunlight crosses the horizon, walk through the arch. Do not look back. Leave the past where it belongs and move onward.

Also, the beaches and countryside of Bermuda are dotted with moongates: round, people-sized limestone carvings. Find one of these and walk through it to improve your good fortune. It's said these work best for honeymooners, who will also receive a life-time of love.

Side Trips   There are a lot of sites you'll want to take in during your trip. Go to the crystal caves, a striking exhibit of stalagmites and stalactites formed out of limestone, some of which even glow. These are on the east end of the island near Harrington Sound. Right nearby you'll also discover Devil's Hole, a collapsed cave that is now a fish and turtle preserve. The admission here is $5 for adults, and $3 for children (open March to October). Or, visit the Botanical Gardens in Hamilton, just fifteen minutes away from your cottage. Here you'll find twenty different areas with more flowers than you can count, including an orchid exhibit, a bamboo grove, and a tea garden.

NIAGARA FALLS, NEW YORK
Elements: Water, air
Themes: Courage, cleansing, communication, energy

Niagara Falls is located in both the United States and Canada, on the eastern end of Lake Erie, just north of Buffalo, New York, via the Robert Moses Parkway. Because it is a major tourist attraction, there are numerous hotels, restaurants, and camping places on both sides of the falls, but the Canadian falls offer a better view and cleaner facilities.

Travel timing is purely personal. In the winter the falls are covered with snow and ice, which are illuminated by colored lamps. This is spectacular, but the weather doesn't always cooperate for long-term viewing. In the summer, it's very refreshing to walk along the falls (which have numerous outlook posts) and take in the cooling spray.

Several tours are available, including one of the Bridal Veil Falls, which actually gets you behind the scenes in the Cave of the Winds. Another is the Maid of the Mist ride at the base of the Horseshoe Falls. Either tour costs about $5 U.S. and is well worth the money. For more information, contact the Niagara Falls Convention and Visitors Bureau at 800-421-5223. On-line information is available through: tourismniagara.com/nfcvcb

History and Folklore Known to the Iroquois as the Thundering Waters, this was an ancient site of worship for the natives who came here to increase their strength and bravery. The first white person to see Niagara Falls was a French missionary in the late 1600s, after being told about the home of the spirits by the natives. Since that time, it has become a well-known tourist attraction and honeymoon retreat.

About This Site It's hard to adequately describe the raw power and beauty of 600,000 gallons of water per second moving downward over a precipice. Even though I live nearby, I never cease being amazed by the site and its effect on everyone who comes to visit. In some spots the thunder of the waves drowns out everything but your own heartbeat and the voice of the goddess, embodied in the water. It's very empowering, especially for someone who's been feeling drained or those suffering from chronic fatigue.

Activities Be forewarned that it's nearly impossible to get much privacy at the falls for spells or rituals, so you'll have to find ways to achieve inner solitude when you're working magic here.

According to custom, if you have a message you wish to convey to someone far away, tell the water. It will carry your words to that person. Or, if you have a pressing question in your heart, whisper it to the current and then listen patiently. The water's voice will return with an answer from the spirits who reside there.

Take a piece of cheesecloth with you when you go and gather water from the natural spray. Wash this over your brow and wipe it across your heart chakra to cleanse away fear and tension, inspire fortitude, and improve your determination for any situation you face.

Finally, just stand and watch the water as it rolls over the falls. There is an immense amount of energy here that you can simply absorb by being nearby and open to it. To improve the effect, give a small gift to the waters (like a bread crumb), as the Iroquois used to do, and pray for the type of energy you most need. Or, release a symbol of a problem you're having to the waters and let the ancient goddess take care of it for you.

PERCE ROCK, GASPE PENINSULA, QUEBEC, CANADA
Elements: Air, earth, water, spirit
Themes: Productivity, ecology, meditation

Perce is located in the gulf of the St. Lawrence River in the eastern Quebec provence. I suggest having a car available, as many neighboring sites and accommodations are somewhat spread out through wide-open lands that are perfect for slow, thought-provoking, inspiring drives.

If you don't mind the cold, you might want to try traveling in February for the Quebec Winter Carnival that features ice sculptures, illuminated snow castles, winter sports, and many other activities throughout the provence. For more information, contact the Quebec Tourism Department at 800-363-7777, or on-line at quebecweb.com/tourisme/quebec.

History and Folklore   Gaspe was one of the first tourist regions in Quebec because of its coastal panorama and terrific salmon fishing. It was named after the French Canadian writer Philippe Gaspe, who made his estate on the St. Lawrence River. According to tradition, Gaspe wrote his nostalgic novel *Anciens Canadiens* after years of meditation and research.

About This Site   The Gaspe Peninsula has a variety of cultural influences, which makes it colorful, interesting, and lovely. The combination of Appalachian hills and lowland makes for some incredible sightseeing, especially of Perce Rock itself, which juts up out of the water as if from nowhere to touch the bright blue sky.

The top of the rock is a bird sanctuary, so there are literally hundreds of birds flying or landing overhead all the time. When the tide is low, you can walk out and explore the caverns that go through the rock. Afterward, return to land and enjoy some salmon or lobster on an outdoor veranda from one of the local shops.

Activities   By all means, bring some bread crumbs and feed the birds. As you do, impart your wishes to them, especially those that have to do with preserving a treasured project or inspiring fruitfulness in any part of your life.

Enjoy a hearty fish lunch or dinner. Bless the meal so that as you eat it, you can internalize the energy of abundance and fruitfulness that fish represent.

Go to a nearby hillside and look out over the waters as you meditate on earth's beauty and sacredness. Let the wonder of creation fill and hold you. Recognize the Great Spirit's fingerprint on all things as far as your eyes can see, including your heart.

Petrified Forest Park, Arizona
Elements: Water, fire
Themes: Preservation, protection

Located along Interstate 40 just twenty-five miles east of Holbrook, and about five miles from Calistoga Hot Springs, one can see both the Petrified Forest and the Painted Desert (see

"Side Trips"). There is a twenty-plus mile long highway running through the park, with viewing places throughout for passers-through. If you want to go to the main areas only, parking will run you about $5 per vehicle per day.

Since this is a desert, you'll probably want to avoid traveling in mid-summer. No matter when you go, however, you'll be treated to the sight of basketweavers and the work of other Pueblo artists throughout the area. Holbrook (which is the nearest town along I-40) hosts several options for lodging and eating, and a visitor's center that can be reached by calling 520-524-6228. On-line information is available at xray.chm.bris.ac.uk:8000/holiday/ariz/petr.

History and Folklore   The Petrified Forest is composed of stones that began forming around 225 million years ago and are twice as hard as granite. As the name implies, a huge forest once existed here that was later inundated by floods. These waters began preserving the trees with sediment, the minerals slowly replacing wood with stone.

Local folklore claims that anyone taking samples without asking first will receive bad luck because this insults the desert spirits. It's thought that park personnel created this myth to keep souvenir-takers from becoming greedy and ruining the site. Be that as it may, the park receives hundreds of samples back every year, attesting to the power of the legend!

About This Site   The Petrified Forest is an expanse of ancient tree remains that were preserved by time's hands. Along with them, dinosaur bones and numerous other fossils from earth's early history can be found. Vibrant colors and patterns appear throughout the region, resulting from eroded hematite (black), limonite (yellow), and gypsum (white) stone.

Several different mini-sites are mapped out in the park. The Blue Mesa has blue-gray clay, but excessive tourist traffic is discouraged here due to the soil's sensitivity. The Jasper Forest was once comprised of huge logs until early prospectors cleaned most of them out. The Crystal Forest suffered similarly from souvenir hunters who gathered up the quartz- and amethyst-dotted logs before preservation efforts began.

The two best exhibits in the park are the Rainbow Forest and the Agate House. The Rainbow Forest is still fairly intact, housing hundreds of flat-lying sections of petrified wood. The Agate House is a native hut made in the eighteenth century exclusively from petrified wood.

Activities   The gift shop offers a variety of items so you can take a little of the park's energy home with you. Put your chosen trinket with anything that you want to protect and pre-serve for many years (like inside a photo album or with your magical treasures).

If you can watch a sunset here, do so. The mingling of hues as the sun touches the horizon is striking and filled with the fire element. Reach out your hands and let the fires rekindle your spirit for whatever tasks lie ahead.

Side Trips   Adjacent to the Petrified Forest you'll discover the Painted Desert, which got its name because of the oddly col-ored layers of sediment dotting the sand, ranging in hue from purple to gray, orange, and red. The Painted Desert was the site of an ancient ocean that left behind minerals to create canyons of hue that are so breathtaking they seem unnatural. Information on this site is also available through the Holbrook Visitor's Center.

PETRA, JORDAN
Elements: Earth, fire
Themes: Networking, communication, hospitality

Jordan, home to the real Lawrence of Arabia and numerous Biblical stories, is a very welcoming part of the world. It houses numerous sites, including the spectacular city of Petra. Most accommodations can be found on the East Bank plateau, along with beautiful mosques, Roman ruins, crafts, and entertainment from Bedouins who offer music and belly dancers.

Visas for tourism can be issued in advance from the consulate or upon your arrival. You might want to stay in Amman, a good-sized city that's easily accessible to most sites within a few hours. It has a variety of eating and sleeping establishments in almost all price ranges, along with tourist information centers. Amman is approximately 160 miles from Petra via the Desert Highway (about three hour's drive).

You might want to consider traveling in August when the cultural/arts festival takes place, or during November for the water sports competitions. For more information, contact the Jordan Information Bureau at 202-265-1606 or the Jordanian Embassy at 202-966-2664.

History and Folklore   *Petra* means "rock" or "stone," which is not surprising considering its construction. The principal god in the area, Dusares, was himself represented by a stone in which he was believed to dwell. Today Petra is sometimes called the "rose-red city, half as old as time," alluding to its visual impact and ancientness.

The people inhabiting Petra were from a nomadic tribe from northern Arabia. They arrived here around 800 B.C. Over time, the city the Nabataean people established here became a key area in Asia for exchanging both goods and information. From the Gulf to the Dead Sea and from Mesopotamia to Egypt, trade routes developed here, including part of the silk and spice trail that spurred development throughout the region.

About This Site   A rock-cut city located in the desert of Jordan is best known today for the scenery it provided for the film *Indiana Jones and the Last Crusade*. You arrive at the city via a narrow, steep path where rocks known as the *siq* loom overhead. At the end of the road, you'll come to the Khasneh, the best-preserved building, which is cut 100 feet wide and 130 feet tall into the surrounding rocks. The word *Khasneh* means "treasury," which led to wild tales of great treasures hidden within.

The architecture throughout Petra is an odd mingling of Persian, Arabic, Greek, and Assyrian, giving it a striking classical face. It is sometimes called the rose-red city because of the rock's coloration, especially at sunrise and sunset. The layers of color are formed from the stone strata, something the builders were aware of and used effectively.

A brief review of the city's various attributes helps us understand its former glory: huge staircases, arched gates, paved roads, a Roman theater, banquet halls, homes of various sizes, and baths. One feature of particular interest is known simply as "the pool"—a 80,000-plus cubic foot reservoir for water to supply the city. This pool, attached to an aqueduct and pipes, was another reason why Petra thrived as it did in the desert.

Activities   Enjoy a cup of fresh brewed coffee, which is a sacred beverage in Arabic tradition. As you drink it, feel the warmth that welcomes you from within and without. Keep a few coffee beans in your pocket as a charm that inspires hospitality throughout the rest of your travels. Also, carry a pinch of salt; this ensures that you will never overstay your welcome.

Since this area was a historical hub for communication between peoples, gather up a little sand for a personal power pouch and carry it with you when you need your words to be sure and effective. Or, sprinkle a pinch to the winds to help manifest magical networking contacts.

Side Trips   If you enjoy scuba diving, go to the gulf, which is noted for its tropical fish and coral. Or, visit Mount Nebo where Moses surveyed the promised land. And don't forget a walk through the Jordan Valley, where Mohammed crossed into Jerusalem and where you can see the Dome of the Rock.

PETROGLYPH NATIONAL MONUMENT — ALBUQUERQUE,
NEW MEXICO
Element: Varies
Themes: Warmth, momentum, shamanic journeys,
  attraction

The main visitors' center is off Unser Boulevard at Western
Trail near I-40 in Albuquerque. From Unser you can access
hiking trails in addition to finding parking ($1 weekdays, $2
weekends) and picnic areas. This road will also allow you into
Boca Negra Canyon, which is open from 8 to 5 during winter
and 9 to 6 in the summer months. Hotels in all price ranges are
abundant throughout the area, especially on I-40.

Spring is an excellent time to travel, especially in mid-March
when the desert is alive with flowers and animals. Summer isn't
recommended for those sensitive to heat, and the rattlesnakes
can become an issue during hot months.

About This Site   This 7,500-acre site preserves one of the
largest petroglyph regions in North America. It has a 17-mile-
long escarpment containing over 15,000 petroglyphs, adjacent
to 3,400 acres with five major volcanos. This combination makes
for an odd blending of elements. The West Mesa is strongly
earth, with air and fire mingled in due to an abundance of dirt,
rock, ash, sand, birds, and prairie dogs, but the Earth Mother
predominates, the lower you venture into the canyons.

The fire element comes from the volcanoes. Steam vents still
release hot, moist air from deep with the earth's womb. And
even though this is desert, the water element sometimes appears
here, too. The region has several arroyos — decorated with petroglyphs of dragonflies — through which water pours from
higher elevations during rain storms.

Activities   Volcanic rock dusts the land, making everything
somewhat magnetic. This means that you can draw specific

energies to yourself here by carrying an image of what you most need. Alternatively, "warm up" any project or relationship that's grown slightly cold by leaving a biodegradable offering at one of the heat vents.

Many sensitive people find themselves drawn into a light trance state here, making it perfect for shamanic-styled journeys. The volcano region makes the best spot for extended private meditation, especially in Piedras Marcadas, which is also where some Pueblo rituals are held. According to local folklore, the volcanoes are a direct entryway to the upperworld where the Great Spirit dwells.

REDWOODS STATE PARK, CALIFORNIA
Elements: Earth, spirit
Themes: Time, ecology, fairies, connection, growth

The redwoods are located in the Southern Humbolt Park area of California, near Highway 101 and 299. The state park offers camping grounds, bike trails, fishing, swimming, a nature center, and special events yearround. Temperatures in this region range from 53 to 65 degrees Fahrenheit almost consistently. The sunnier times are during mid-spring and mid-fall; otherwise, anticipate a fair amount of rain and pack accordingly.

If you plan to take a tour, I recommend Redwood Exposure, which is an environmentally oriented group with professional naturalists. E-mail them at redwood@northcoat.com, or call 707-839-0216. For other tourism information go to: www.northwest.com/~hrsp/#fac.

History This park has the largest remaining old-growth redwood forest in the United States. In its ancient past the land was engulfed by various fires. This cleared the land for redwood growth and made the perfect soil content so the trees would

thrive. Fires came again later, after the redwoods started taking hold, but they cleared out the underbrush and made small hollows in the trees for wildlife. As a result, there is a plethora of flora and fauna that lives beneath the protective bows of these huge watchtowers.

About This Site Be prepared to feel small. These trees reach hundreds of feet into the sky as if to touch spirit itself. This is a rainforest, filled with mosses, ferns, and mushrooms. The overall first impression is a lot like entering an adventure in a mystical, timeless land. Here you can observe for yourself nature's interrelatedness and progression.

For bird lovers, there are several exotic species that live here, including the brown pelican and great egret. This is likely why several wildlife sanctuaries exist in the area, along with a very active Audubon Society that studies the migrant species.

Activities Take a long hike and watch for a tree bearing an oval or round ring formed around its base out of bark. These rings form whenever the tree is damaged, allowing for new growth, and are charmingly called fairy rings. You may want to leave a small offering here for the fey and the devic spirits of the land.

In addition, sit and meditate beneath a tree. Sense its ancientness—the wisdom it must hold from watching so much history! Allow yourself to meld with the tree, feeling its strong roots beneath you. Reach up to touch the sky and spirit. When you're done, take a small amount of soil from beneath that tree (a pinch will do) and keep it with you to foster personal growth.

Finally, you may want to look into a membership with the park. The monies from memberships go toward conservation efforts and park upkeep.

RIO GRANDE GORGE, NEW MEXICO
Elements: Earth, water, fire
Themes: Energy, healing, perspective

The Rio Grande Gorge (and many other wonderful sites in New Mexico) is located just outside Taos along the Santa Fe Trail. This city is known for its magical "hum" (an underlying throbbing or vibration) and offers a wide variety of accommodations and tourist services, including bed-and-breakfast lodging, resorts, whitewater rafting, and spas. Note, however, that the U.S. Congress has limited access to certain parts of the gorge to protect its forty-seven miles of wilderness

A great deal of local information is available on the Web at www.taoswebb.com, riogrande.net.mx, or www.newmexiconet. com. Otherwise, call the Tourism Division at 1-800-545-2040.

History and Folklore   The Rio Grande is an ancient huge cut in the earth's stone that begins in Colorado, slowly deepening to 800 feet. There is one charming local story about a point that overlooks the Rio Grande Gorge State Park from the East. It's called Outlaw Hill, and it claims the dubious honor of having desperados regularly hide out there. Apparently, the hill is perfectly located to watch for the long-arm of the law while resting from hasty retreats.

About This Site   Taos has been the focal point of a lot of New Age attention because it seems to be centered amid several important sacred sites, including the oldest inhabited native pueblo. It is, in fact, called the "Soul of the Southwest." The energy in this area is so potent that spiritually sensitive people often complain of hearing a constant throbbing or ringing sound that they can't shake throughout their visit. The Rio Grande region is no exception.

The Rio Grande Gorge represents a huge tear in the earth's crust that lies far beneath what our eyes can see. The waters that flow here begin in the Sangre de Cristo Mountains, slowly carving out this haven for hawks and eagles as well as many other forms of wildlife. In contrast to the stone and water, conifer forests cover half the region, along with long-forgotten Indian ruins.

Activities   Go to Outlaw Hill and think of a situation in your life that needs healing. Hold a pebble in your hand as you focus any residual anger or negativity into the stone. Release it over the edge, and with it release yourself to begin anew. Let this place provide refreshed perspectives.

Alternatively, find a fairly private spot to sit and simply attune yourself to the abundant vibrations here. At first they might feel a little itchy on your senses, and you'll want to filter out all but what you most need. When you're done, you might find that the energy leaves you tingly and a bit high strung because of its intensity, so take a long walk to ground yourself again and enjoy the improved sensual input it provides.

Side Trips   Make sure you go through the town of Arroyo Hondo. Just outside are the Black Rock and Manby Hot Springs, which will restore your health and invigorate your aura. These "clothing-optional" springs remain at a nearly constant temperature of 97 degrees, and they are among the most scenic in all of New Mexico. Some say that the series of seven hot springs here, each of which is a little harder to get to than the last, represents the chakras. By going to each, you slowly traverse your own physical/spiritual nature through the energy points and open the crown chakra to receive enlightenment.

ROCK OF APHRODITE, CYPRESS
Elements: Water, earth
Themes: Love, passion, protection

Cyprus has numerous hotels and resorts. One region that you might want to consider staying at is Pafos, which is only twenty-five kilometers away from the Rock of Aphrodite. Pafos is one of the legal ports of entry, and one of the safest, to Cyprus. It has an international airport for your traveling convenience, a stunning harbor, an archaeological museum, and numerous other sacred sites nearby for your enjoyment.

For more information, refer to www.kypros.org/cytprus/tourist, cosmosnet.net/azias/cyprus, or call the Cyprus tourist organization at 212-683-5280.

History and Folklore   Known locally as Petra Tou Romiou, Aphrodite's Rock is but one of the many sites that give Cyprus a feeling of antiquity and immense visual appeal. As an important Mediterranean trading post that brought Asia and Europe together, Cypress's shores saw many culturally diverse visitors and much prosperity before the tidal wave of A.D. 364 that destroyed much of its former glory.

In Greek mythology it was here that the gods and goddesses came to indulge in sports, and where Aphrodite emerged from the sea's foam at Pafos to become one of the most important divine figures in history. Aphrodite is the goddess of love, passion, and beauty, and her touch resonates through the island, thanks to the thousands of people who worshiped in this exact spot.

About This Site   Cypress appears to be the land that time forgot. Its character is shaped by a natural loveliness from beaches, craggy coasts, hills, and green forests. Amid this striking scenery stands Petra Tou Romiou (Rock of the Greek) right near where the goddess rose from the waters. This particular landmark is also associated with a frontier guard from Byzantine times, Dighenis Akritas, who kept the Saracens away by heaving a large rock (Petra) at them.

Activities   Stand at the shoreline looking at the goddess's image in nature. Tell her where your relationships seem to be wanting, and toss a rose upon the water as a wish for love to return to you on her blue waves. Or, if you have need of strength or protection, seek out the energy left behind by the hero Dighenis Akritas.

Or go to Kouklia village (fourteen kilometers away from Paphos), which was one of the ancient Greek pilgrimage sites. The ruins here date back to the twelfth century B.C. and bear the energy imprint of both the goddess and the devout who came here to pay homage and pray. There is no reason not to follow their example.

Side Trips   Visit the Ayia Solomoni Church on St. Paul Street. There is a tree here that, according to local tradition, will cure disease for those who hang an offering from its bows. Or, in keeping with our theme, further away, about forty-five kilometers north of Paphos you can visit Aphrodite's Baths. The goddess herself was said to wash here in a natural grotto shaded by fig trees.

SAINTES MARIES DE LA MER, FRANCE
Elements:Water, fire
Themes: Renewal, hospitality

This simple village of fishing families is located on the south-central coast of France. Staying in the town itself has a lot of advantages from a cultural standpoint, but if you want "fancier," the closest city with charm and a good variety of accommodations is Marseille. Marseille lies about an hour away from the region of Camargue, on a hill overlooking the French coast, fields of lavender, and groves of olive trees. The city is dotted with both medieval fortresses and Roman ruins, to occupy your free time. Other neat sites here include a tapestry museum, Fountain of the Nine Cannons and Thermal Water, various abbeys, and much more.

Time your trip for the month of July when you'll be treated to the entire village igniting with the sound of flamenco music and dancing. Or, come in May for the festival that celebrates the saints whose bones rest here (see "History and Folklore"). France has several good Web sites to refer to, including france-tourism.com and fgtousa.org. Alternatively, call the French Government Tourist Office at 212-838-7800 for more information.

History and Folklore This ornithological park is a very sacred place for gypsies. It is said that St. Sarah, the patroness of gypsies, was shipwrecked near here and died in the town itself. Her remains are kept in the fifteenth-century church of Les Saintes Maries. Gypsies consider it an honor to visit here at least once in a lifetime. The gypsies were not the only ones to venerate this region, however. The list includes the Celts and Romans. Apparently, this was a place of worship for the Celtic water goddess and the Roman Mithras, making for an interesting blend of water-fire.

Today this port town is popular for veil sailing (planchists), as the wind here is ideal attaining for record-breaking speed.

About This Site   The people of Saintes Maries de la Mer have deliberately kept their town from appearing touristy, much to their credit. The village looks unassuming and quiet, despite the fact that it has a four-star hotel and other modern lodging establishments. The architects here insisted on traditional style, so nothing looks out of place.

Activities   Go to the church and look at the Sara-la-Kali image. This woman's image is thought to be that of an ancient pagan goddess who welcomed travelers and eased their fatigue. Say a prayer for a trip filled with hospitality, offer a flower as a gift, and leave trusting that your prayer will be answered.

If you find yourself unwell when you arrive in the town or have had troubles along the way, touching any of the saint's images at the church is said to bring instant healing and remove all obstacles in your path.

Finally, you may want to gather up some seawater if you're visiting during the May 25 festival. During this time of year, the water is considered to be blessed by the presence of the saint, and therefore it makes a powerful component for future healing spells or rituals for revitalization.

Side Trips   France has many sacred places, perhaps most notably Notre Dame, the Arc de Triomphe, and the French Pompeii. One of the closest of particular interest for healing magic is Le Puy en Velay in Haute-Loire, just north of Saintes Maries de la Mer. Here you'll find a pilgrimage point where people visited a druidic fever stone thought to cure many maladies.

Any of these sites is worth the trip, as is a brief jaunt to a vineyard to stock up on ritual wine!

SALEM, MASSACHUSETTS
Element: Water
Themes: Emotional healing, witchcraft

The city of Salem hosts a wide variety of accommodations for tourists, including hotels, bed-and-breakfast facilities, an amusement park, and a maritime museum. Information about the city, accommodations, and the like can be obtained through City Hall at 978-745-9595, the Salem Tourism Office at 800-777-6848, or by visiting their Web site at www.salemweb.com. General information about Massachusetts is available through the Office of Travel and Tourism at 800-447-6277 or www.magnet.state.ma.us/travel.

History and Folklore   Best known for the witch trials of 1692, for whatever reason Salem became the center of the witch hysteria in the United States that similarly occurred in Europe. By the time things finally calmed down, twenty-four people had been put to death by torture, hanging, stoning, or imprisonment. Over five hundred documents about the trials are stored in the Peabody Museum, along with objects like witch pins that were used to examine suspected witches.

Since those horrible times Salem has recovered from its past and has become a mecca for witches, complete with a Witch Museum; a Witch Village, where people can learn facts about Wicca; various Wiccan/pagan educational organizations; and several well-known witches living in the city. In effect, Salem's history inspired an atmosphere of tolerance, showing us that we can learn from our mistakes!

About This Site   Over one-third of Salem is park land, and over eighteen miles of it skirt the Atlantic Ocean, making for beautiful beaches and lovely greenery, along with the rich history that's all around. Salem has an odd mingling of old and new: colonial and early Victorian buildings, a pioneer village, picnic areas, horses and buggies that regularly are driven through town, pirate relics, and open-air marketplaces.

There's even a tall ship in the harbor, a reconstructed version of the 171-foot ship built in 1797. Known as the *Friendship*, this boat originally traveled old-world routes, gathering up exotic spices, sugar, and coffee from around the globe until it was captured by the British in 1812.

Activities   Much will depend on the time of year when you travel. Should you come on Samhain (Halloween) or winter solstice, you'll be able to partake of the annual open circles held by PRANCE (Pagan Resource and Network Council of Educators, 94 Derby St., Suite 9, Salem, MA 01970).

At other times of the year, make sure to stop for a while at the Witch Trials Memorial (Charter Street). This site, dedicated in memory of the 300th anniversary of the trial, was created to inspire respect toward people of all paths and bring to bear what the phrase "never again, the burning" means in our society. The people who died here, most of whom probably weren't Wiccan, paved the way for our freedom. Pray for their spirit's peace.

Side Trips   Salem has a lot of sites, which will easily fill a week's vacation. The Peabody Essex Museum (800-745-4054) reflects eighteenth- and nineteenth-century New England. The House of the Seven Gables (978-744-0991) was the mansion made famous by Nathaniel Hawthorne. Witch House (which was the seventeenth-century residence of trial judge Jonathan Corwin) is the only home still standing with direct ties to the witch trials (978-744-0180), and the Witch Museum honors our past (978-744-1692). There's even whale watching down at the port (978-741-0434), and while you are here, you can shop 'til you drop!

SAUT D'EAU, HAITI
Element: Water
Themes: Healing, passion, luck, magic

Saut D'Eau is located in the village of Bonheur just north of Port-au-Prince, Haiti. You'll likely want to find accommodations in Port-au-Prince, the capital city, where a great deal of the Haitian culture is more than evident, including the mysteries of voodoo, a unique blending of Catholicism, magic, and ritual. This city offers open-air markets, beaches, coral reefs, and hotels. However, because of recent civil unrest, even the best hotels sometimes experience power outages and roads are in poor repair. For the same reason, it is not advisable to walk in the city after dark, and your valuables should be safely hidden or locked up at all times.

From the city you can take Route National 3 into Bonheur. Many people walk or ride a donkey down this road rather than take transportation, as a kind of offering to the goddess who resides there. Guides are available for about $20 a day.

Mid-July marks the traditional pilgrimage, if you want to time your visit accordingly. Pack for temperatures of about 80 degrees. To get an update on the political atmosphere or more information, call the State Overseas Citizens Service at 202-647-5225, or the Haitian Embassy 202-332-4090.

History and Folklore   Columbus discovered Haiti in 1492. In the seventeenth century, Haiti came under French rule; they managed to build the country considerably. In 1804, a civil dispute led to Haiti becoming the world's first black republic. Up until recently, political upheaval has been a nearly continual facet of Haitian life, but it could not overcome the natural beauty of this place or the magical powers of many of its sites.

Among these, we find Saut D'Eau, an incredibly beautiful waterfall dedicated to the Vodoun goddess Elizi (Erzulie), associated with health, love, sexuality, luck, magic, and, of course, water!

About This Site   Port-au-Prince has many sites to fill your time. Begin at the Centre d'Art and view colorful bits of Haitian history done in French creole style. Move on to the Cathedral of Sainte Trinite and stop at the Iron Market, where merchants sell a marvelous assortment of handicrafts. Or, travel uphill to the Barbancourt Rum Distillery so you can taste this nectar firsthand, which also has ritual uses as a libation and aspurger.

Route National 3 takes a few zigs and zags on its way to Bonhour, but, all things considered, it's in fairly good condition. The falls themselves have a mystical appeal, being thirty meters of gushing water overhung with creepers, surrounded by shallow pools, and edged in sheets of limestone.

Activities   Voodoo tradition says to come and bathe in the water by candlelight. Bring an offering for the spirit who abides there to encourage improved luck, healing, or sex appeal. Suitable gifts include fresh bananas, salt water, or blue items.

Take the opportunity to learn more about voodoo beliefs and practices and consider some of their similarities to Wicca. In this manner we can begin to see how people are more alike than different, at least spiritually. In voodoo there is one god, but many spirits who can help with daily life. The ancestors also hold an important place here, watching specifically over their families (like guides or guardian angels). Drums are used to aid the trance state of worshipers, herbalism is an important healing art, and spirits can communicate through individuals (similar to channeling and mediumship).

Side Trips   Go to Plaine du Nord, a farming community that houses the Church of Saint James. When it rains here, people gather up the mud to also gather the power of Ogou, a deity who can improve fertility, grant blessings, and heal, if properly appeased. Suitable offerings include prayers, candles, coins, and rum.

For more information on this site, and all of Haiti, look to www.haitionline.com.

SERPENT MOUND STATE MEMORIAL, OHIO
Elements: Earth, fire
Themes: Universal brotherhood, change

The Great Serpent Earth Mound slithers neatly near Route 73 deep in the Ohio River Valley. The cities of Columbus, Reynolds-burg, and Logan are all within an hour's drive of the site and offer the best potential accommodations and camping facilities.

The park is open to visitors yearround from 10 A.M. until 4 P.M. Parking is $5; bikers and walkers only pay $1. Specific information may be obtained through the Ohio Historical Society at 614-466-1500, or the Ohio Tourism Department at 800-282-5393. On-line information is available by viewing www.ohiohistory.org

History and Folklore   The serpent was carefully formed near a meteorite crater by the hands of Adena Indians, who left behind few indications of how they achieved this wonder. We do know, however, that the site wasn't inhabited—it was, instead, a place for ritual and worship.

One legend claims that the local Indians made the snake to honor a lunar eclipse, which would be in keeping with snakes as the guardians of celestial happenings. It also might have com-memorated the meteorite crash, considering the mound dates to about 1200 B.C. Another story tells us that the mound was con-structed because of the recurring odd events that reveal the land's life-essence, like the 1975 report of leaves coming to life without a wind to aid them.

Because of the snake's bite, it has some correlation with the fire element, but living so close to the soil it cannot help but symbolize earth, too. Other shamanic associations for the snake symbol include passion, vitality, creativity, comprehension, and the ability to transmute the energy in any of these things for positive personal changes or achievements.

About This Site   One of the most famous earth mounds in the United States, this serpent stretches itself across thousands of feet of land, making for an impressive site from the air. You can see it from the ground, too, if an air tour isn't your cup of tea. From either location, the twining image of a snake, holding an egg in its mouth, is unmistakable.

It is but one of many such patterns throughout the woods near the Little Miami River, all of which were designed by natives to tell a story and commemorate animal spirits who helped guide their lives.

Activities   The park includes a trail that goes completely around the snake. It is well worth your time to walk the distance, thinking as you go about what message the snake spirit holds for your life. What do you need to change? What have you done recently to reconnect yourself with the music of the spheres and the universe's voice?

Come nightfall, you can't stay in the park but you can stand outside nearby, gaze at the stars, and recognize yourself as a citizen of eternity. Close your eyes and visualize the snake as made out of stars, then let that transformational light seep into your soul.

Side Trips   There are numerous mounds, pictographs, and historical sites in this region or within a reasonable driving distance. The Adam's County information line is 800-752-2757.

SHASTA, CALIFORNIA
Elements: Air, fire
Themes: Longevity, spirituality, healing, vitality

Mount Shasta is located in Siskiyou County of California, with the town of Shasta directly below it. Here you can find a good

variety of lodging and other amenities, including sporting goods stores.

The mountain offers all types of skiing and snowmobile outings during the winter months. If winter sports aren't your strong suit, try to travel in the spring when the full moon is in Taurus. This is when the Mount Shasta festival of the Buddha is held with a plethora of interesting events and pageantry.

For more information, contact the Division of Tourism at 800-862-2543 or via the internet at www.gocalif.ca.gov.

History and Folklore As a volcano that's erupted in relatively recent history (about two hundred years ago), Mount Shasta has incited many myths and legends. For example, some people believe there's an underground city here called Telos where over one million inhabitants live vastly extended lives.

A Native-American myth tries to explain why the volcano erupted by telling us that the great trickster spirit, the Coyote, used to live here. One day he was very hungry so he visited the Shasta Indians to ask for some salmon. When the village said it was okay, the Coyote took far more than he needed, making for a heavy load. On the way home, the Coyote moved slowly. Swarms of bees came in and before he could do anything, they ate all but the fish's bones! When Coyote got another load of fish, he enlisted the aid of the Shasteans to protect his catch. When the bees succeeded again, they were followed to the top of Mount Shasta where they took the salmon deep into the mountain's mouth as if feeding it.

Coyote then had an idea. He would have the Shasteans build a big fire and smoke the bees out. They carefully plugged up all the holes in the mountain and began feeding in the smoke through the top and then capping that entrance as well. Coyote and the Indians then heard a deep rumbling from within. The top of the mountain burst open from the smoke, spewing cooked salmon everywhere! And that is how Mount Shasta became an active volcano.

About This Site   This huge volcano looms over 14,000 feet in the air, making it one of the most visible peaks in California. The beauty of the mountain is difficult to overlook, with bits of white, brown, and green creating a mosaic against the blue sky. Above and beyond the striking imagery, there is a definite energy vortex here, and people regularly report UFO sightings in this region.

Activities   The base of Mount Shasta is home to several New Age groups including the Brotherhood of the White Temple and a Zen monastery. You'll want to explore the local yellow pages and see if there are any groups whose activities or centers might interest you.

Stand at the base of the mountain and embrace its essence. The energy here inspires awakening, aliveness, and wholeness in anyone who seeks it. Note that this energy seems to experience shifts, depending on the time of day. Dawn renews hope, noon revitalizes personal and spiritual energy, dusk brings inner knowingness, and night inspires rest in the most restless of hearts.

Side Trips Perhaps the most beautiful view of Mount Shasta and the surrounding area is obtained by air on a hot balloon ride (this gives a whole new meaning to connecting with the air element!). These are available through Shasta Valley Balloon rides, 530-926-3612 or e-mail: balloons@inreach.com.

SHWE DAGON, MYANMAR
Element: Fire
Themes: Joy, passion, health, prayer

Formerly known as Burma, Myanmar is often called the Golden Land because of its ornate temples. This term, however, might be better applied to the Myanmar people, whose hospitality, happiness, and genuine warmth are world-renowned. Nonetheless, you'll need a tourist visa from the Myanmar Embassy, along with your passport, when you land.

It's suggested that you stay in Yangon (Rangoon), the capital city, which houses the Shwe Dagon Pagoda along with many other sight-seeing attractions such as the National Museum, a zoo, and a sacred cave. Airlines go directly into Yangon, and taxis are available from there to your hotel or other locations.

In terms of travel times, well . . . there's always a party going on in Myanmar, but March is the official Shwe Dagon Pagoda Festival, which includes some of the world's best dancers. April offers the New Year's festival, where water is splashed all over everyone to clean out the old and welcome the new. Unfortunately, these are also the hottest months of the year, often very rainy, so pack accordingly. For more information, call the Myanmar Embassy at 202-332-9044.

History and Folklore The Shwe Dagon has been in this land for over 1,000 years as a testament to these people's firm and devout Buddhist beliefs. Even so, around the inside of the pagoda you'll find statues of beings called *Nats*, a kind of nature spirit, and little bells to get their attention. These beings are said to protect the temple and its worshipers almost as much as the Buddha does!

The pagoda was renovated in the late 1700s with monumental efforts, including raising the mound, resurfacing, and gold leafing. Shwe Dagon remains the world's tallest religious building, and one of the best maintained. Each year pilgrims come to add more gold leaf to the shrine because it is here, suitably, that relics of the Gautama Buddha and three other Buddhas before him are said to be housed.

About This Site   Shwe Dagon is a feast for one's eyes, especially the main bell-shaped stupa, which has lotus blossom wreathes, umbrellas with rubies and diamonds, and all other manner of adornment. In front of this you'll get to see the Shwe Dagon Bell, one of the largest bells in the world. In addition, the pagoda itself has over 100 gold and 1,400 silver bells around it, all of which call the faithful to prayer.

The pagoda stands almost 300 feet high, with adjacent smaller pagodas all around it like petals on a flower. The entry fee is about $5 U.S. Within a five-minute walk, south of the main site, you'll find another unique pagoda that has a lake out front and a ceiling covered with constellations.

Activities   It's interesting that *Yangon* means "end of conflict." Perhaps your time at the pagoda can be spent in quiet prayer and meditation to find peace within yourself and quiet your mind momentarily.

Traditional offerings here include lotus blossoms, rice, and gold leaf packets, all of which you can buy from vendors nearby. Take these to a suitable location, perhaps beneath the statue of the Buddha who marks your astrological sign, as a way of inspiring good health for the rest of the year.

Finally, observe the people of this area and learn from them the lesson of joyful, worshipful living. In the odd combination of simplicity and pageantry, one can see that spirituality need not be separate from daily living, at least not in Myanmar!

Side Trips   One cannot travel to Burma without seeing the Kyaiktyo Shrine. Here, a huge golden boulder balances on the edge of a precipice. Buddhists make regular pilgrimages to the rock, believing it improves karma, increases joyful living, and aids in fulfilling one's spiritual quest in this life. The rock has been covered in gold leaf as a kind of offering by the faithful — giving the most precious metal on earth to ensure a better life in the hereafter.

SLEEPING GIANT, CONNECTICUT
Elements: Earth, water
Themes: Sleep magic, banishing greed, spiritual counsel

You will find this inspiring natural ridge about five miles north of New Haven via Route 10. A small variety of lodging, food, regional guides, and other amenities are available in New Haven and the neighboring town of Hamden, which is even closer to the site.

The park has numerous hiking trails that offer the avid botany student a feast for the eyes, marking all the interesting plants along the way. (Note: no cars are allowed on hiking trails.) There is also rock climbing, fishing, and a 1.5-mile trail that leads to Mount Carmel, affording a wonderful bird's-eye view.

In terms of travel time, consider coming at the end of May for the Sleeping Giant Bird Watching Exposition and Fair. More information can be obtained through the Park Association at 203-789-7498, the Connecticut Tourism Division at 800-282-6863, or the New Haven Visitor's Bureau at 800-332-7829.

History and Folklore   History tells us of a time long ago when volcanic activity created the unusual land mass that bears an unmistakable human shape (note that this may provide an underlying fire element with which to work). People throughout this area regard the giant as having a very real spirit with a protective personality that watches over the entire Connecticut River Valley. Such animistic views likely stem from the underground water that echoes on the trails below the giant, which residents consider his life's blood.

Native Americans have another interesting outlook. Apparently, a greedy chieftain went to the seashore for fish and ate so much that he fell asleep. Some passing mischievous land spirit then cast a spell on him, and he sleeps still! If you look very hard, it's said the chieftain has great riches in his pockets, which explains the presence nearby of valuable silver and gold mines along with quartz.

About This Site   This human-shaped piece of basalt is over 200 acres in area and over 700 feet high. From a distance, it looks much like a huge man, lying on his back from east to west, foot to head, as if staring at the sky. Nearby there are some large boulders called Giant's Kettles. These are made from rocks different than the native soil, alluding to a deposit by glaciers.

Activities   To this day, the top of the mountain is home to tribal spirits where anyone can come to get sound advice from the voice of the ages. Sit here quietly at sundown and listen to the sounds around you. In the voice of the wind, the song of the waters, and the chime of the sunlight dancing off the land, you'll hear the message or advice you most need.

Besides the flora and fauna, the Sleeping Giant has lovely waterfalls where you can leave behind any sense of avarice, greed, or desire for things that you really *don't* need. Just toss in a small pebble named after the thing(s) for which you mistakenly yearn and let the water carry that unwanted desire away.

And for those reading this who have trouble sleeping, collect a stone or a little soil from the region and put it under your pillow (but make sure it's only a little bit—you don't want to sleep as long as this fellow).

Side Trips   There are wonderful sights to see and activities to enjoy throughout the area; this includes taking the Essex riverboat ride, having a glass of wine at the Clinton Vineyards, and viewing the seventeenth-century sundial gardens in Higganum.

STONE FOREST, BULGARIA
Elements: Water, earth
Themes: Sacred dancing, foundations, fairies

The stone forest of Bulgaria is located just twenty kilometers west of Varna, which is the perfect spot for a vacation for any reason. As a port city on the Black Sea, it has a beautiful mixture of Old World and New World flavor, complete with everything from Greek architecture and industrial parks to fishing and water sports! You'll have no trouble finding suitable accommodations in your price range somewhere in the city.

It's best to travel between May and September, as winter can be cold and rather dreary. For more information, refer to www.bulgaria.com or call 800-852-0944.

History and Folklore   Bulgaria is a land rich in folkloric heritage, including lyrical songs and fairy tales. Part of this tradition emerges in Varna itself because of its unique location, having been a trading post between Constantinople, Venice, and other important points. Some of the other regional myths were likely inspired by the numerous sacred sites, including the stone forest, that dot the land, reminding people of ancient times and mysterious peoples.

Some people claim the stone forest was created when certain people (or fairies) were dancing wildly in the area. The regional spirits were so angered by the dancers' irreverence that they were turned to stone, creating a circular gathering of collumbodies that remain to this day.

About This Site   The stone forest dates to about fifty million years ago. Some of the stone columns in this enigmatic forest reach up to 7 meters in height and 3 meters around (this gives a whole new meaning to the pagan concept of hugging trees!).

When you first pass the sight, you would think it is a ruined temple, but it isn't a temple or a forest at all. Actually, the area is covered with stalagmites formed in an ancient sandstone-bottomed sea. Be that as it may, the energy here definitely speaks of a natural temple in the spiritual sense.

Activities   It might be neat to go here at night and perform a sacred dance that would please the regional spirit. Move gently between the stones, and listen to their voice. Touch them and know their song. As you hear that music, move to it, and become one with the sacredness of this spot.

Because of the earth energies embodied by the stone, mingled with the ancient water here, this is an excellent site for performing spells designed to build foundations under your dreams. Bring a small handful of tiny, tumbled crystals with you. Meditate with them, thinking about all of your hopes and wishes. Then scatter them clockwise to the earth, letting the stones gather them in and give your magic a substructure in which to manifest.

Side Trips   Varna will keep a visitor happily busy for a while. You can visit the nineteenth-century Cathedral of the Assumption of the Virgin and use it as a focus to honor the Goddess. Or, visit the local botanical garden, which houses some wonderful examples of local flora.

SUMMUM PYRAMID, UTAH
Elements: Spirit, earth, air
Themes: Religious studies, unity, meditation

The Summum Pyramid is located in Salt Lake City, making it easily accessible. You'll have no trouble whatsoever finding accommodations in Salt Lake, let alone numerous other sites to enjoy such as canyons, garden tours, and fifteen parks and monuments within but a day's drive of the city.

The visitor's bureau is available at 800-521-2822 (or www.saltlake.org), or you can call the pyramid (located at 707 Genesee Avenue) directly at 801-355-0137.

History and Folklore   The Summum Pyramid was modeled after those in Egypt and Mexico. It was completed in 1979 to act as a temple and a spiritual center. It's interesting to note that it was used as a winery for a short time before the Mormon Church issued a decree that forbade the use of alcohol in worship.

Today the pyramid is a center for people studying Summum philosophy, in which the laws of nature are sacred and religious focus is something encouraged in all peoples. Summum is very tolerant in its outlook, feeling that all are one (which mirrors the Federation of Pagans' motto of Unity through Diversity). This philosophy and way of living also stresses the use of the mind and science to help unravel the mysteries of creation and the cosmos. The word *summum* even means "the sum total of all creation."

About This Site   The pyramid measures 40 feet long and stands 26 feet high, and is aligned with true north as if pointing the way for spiritual seekers to find their path. At the apex of the four corners are huge quartz crystals that have been cut specifically to create the resonance of harmony and to vibrate with the music of the universe itself (thus, the spirit element). Being located in Salt Lake, the underlying energies here are very earthy and cleansing.

Activities   When visiting the site, take a good book with you whose contents you really want to internalize. Ask the Great Spirit (or your personal vision of the god/dess) to guide your eyes to the parts you most need and to make them live in your heart.

Traditionally, this is also a meditative center. Take the opportunity to pause from sightseeing for a while, and have a conversation with your soul. As you meditate, focus wholly on the breath of life and how it connects you to all things, especially the earth spirit. Write down any observations you have afterward in your travel journal or personal diary.

Side Trips   See Zion National Park, an ancient home to the Anaszi Indians and a place still held in regard by numerous tribes. According to native beliefs many spirits live here, and Zion is a perfect location to reconnect with the ancestors. It's quite a ways from Salt Lake, so give yourself plenty of driving time or plan on staying overnight nearby. Specific information is available through the Park's Division at 801-586-7696.

SUNSET CRATER VOLCANO, ARIZONA
Elements: Fire, earth
Themes: Ancestry, shamanic paths

Sunset Crater Volcano is located off U.S. 89 in Flagstaff, Arizona. It is open year-round and offers a visitor's center for information. The last posted entrance fee was $3 per person (children under sixteen are free).

This is a major attraction in the Flagstaff region, which has plentiful accommodations and tour buses for travelers. The park, however, does not, so bring food and beverages. If you want to camp, there is space across from the Visitor's Center at the park for $10 per night.

Depending on the time of travel, weather conditions vary, so call ahead. In July, Flagstaff has a grand arts festival, and the Hopi hold Kachina dances. Other Hopi festivals take place intermittently throughout the year.

You can obtain more information through the Hopi Cultural Center (602-734-2401), the U.S. Forest Service at 520-526-0866, or the Flagstaff Visitor's Center at 800-842-7293.

History and Folklore Sunset Crater Volcano erupted in 1065 when the natives were still living in pit houses as farmers. Those who moved out of the lava's grasp became the cliff dwellers at Walnut Canyon, building their homes with sandstone and mud on the outcroppings.

Traditionally, this entire region was (and is) home to the Hopi and Pueblo people, who practiced rituals here for centuries. The crater itself is still sacred to the Pueblo as a place to commune with the ancestors, and many Hopi trace their clan lineage to this and neighboring sites.

About This Site While you cannot bike or hike on the volcano's main cone, which rises upward 1,000 feet, there are some cinder cones that you can climb to attune with the ancient fire element. In addition, the park has several beautiful trails that you can hike—in particular, Lava Flow Trail, which takes under an hour.

Besides the crater itself, you can see pueblo cliff dwellings that are perfectly preserved, along with the Painted Desert at the nearby Wupatki National Monument and prehistoric cave dwellings at Walnut Canyon.

Activities   If you're camping in the park, consider having a small fire ritual (a contained candle is recommended for safety) at night in which you welcome and honor your own ancestors. To prepare for this, bring pictures with you and meditate on what you feel these people gave you. Place the pictures around the ritual space to welcome the spirits. Also, leave out a gift of food, something they enjoyed in life, to encourage them to join you.

Side Trip   While you're in the area, you may also wish to see Meteor Crater, thirty-five miles east of Flagstaff on I-40. This measures over a mile wide and provides the visitor with the chance to connect with cosmic energies from long ago.

TALLULAH GORGE, GEORGIA
Elements: Water, earth
Themes: Stone magic, meditation

Tallulah Gorge is located directly off Interstate 441, which has several exits into the park, depending on which part you want to visit. The gorge is open daily until dark, with the campgrounds remaining open until 10 P.M. The park has facilities for tents ($10 per night), trailers ($12 per night), picnics, swimming, and hiking, including a 1.5-mile nature trail. Please note that the park has recently instituted new safety rules and requires a permit to descend into the bottom of the gorge.

For ease of access you might want to consider staying in Tallulah Falls or Clayton, which is just a short drive to the

north. A good time to travel is October for the annual Harvest Festival. Detailed information can be obtained by calling 706-754-7970, the Georgia State Park and Historic Site Department at 404-656-3530, or the park superintendent at 706-754-7495.

History and Folklore Despite the fact that Tallulah is Georgia's newest state park, the energy is not new to the Cherokee people who once lived throughout the region. In years gone by, this was a favorite vacation destination for travelers, who considered it so lovely as to nickname it the "Niagara of the South."

The expanse of the gorge has attracted many adventure seekers, two of whom succeeded in crossing it. Unfortunately, after the dam was completed in 1912, many of the falls dried up, taking tourism with them. Thankfully, in recent years, preservation programs have gone into place, including an interpretive center that describes the gorge's history, wildlife, and other regional information.

About This Site   Tallulah Gorge lies between Atlanta and the Smoky Mountains, dropping down over 1,000 feet. Because of the abundant waterfalls and the nearby lake, the energy here is very watery. The gorge itself vibrates with earth (being made of granite), but at a higher speed due to the water's inspiration.

Activities   Friends of mine who traveled here recommend taking a personal staff or wand and dipping it in the water to energize it. This will be even more potent if the wand/staff has water-related wood as a base or decorations, like willow wood, which is considered elementally aligned with water.

Also, find a rock that seems to call to you and sit down for a while to meditate. Lore has it that many of these stones house spirits who will tell you a story if you listen.

TARA HILL AND NEW GRANGE, IRELAND
Elements: Earth, fire
Themes: Cycles, sun magic, fairies, leadership, fertility

Nestled in the heart of the Boyne valley are more than thirty prehistoric monuments, including New Grange and Tara Hill. To visit New Grange, you'll have to go to the visitor's center, as no unaccompanied tours are allowed. Admission runs between $5–$10 U.S. depending on the exchange value of the pound.

If possible, consider coming at winter solstice when the morning rays (about 9 A.M.) of the sun align with a box in the roof here, illuminating the tomb below for twenty minutes. This is the only natural light the chamber receives. Considering the magical significance of the solstice, this seems fitting—bringing light to the darkness.

You will be able to find all kinds of bed-and-breakfast facilities, hotels, and guest houses throughout Meath County. There are hotels due north in Dublin, and the closest town, Drogheda, has a variety of accomodations. For more travel information, refer to www.ireland.travel, call the Navan Traveler's Bureau at 011-353-1-046-73426, New Grange proper 011-353-1-041-24488, or the Irish Tourist Board at 800-223-6470.

History and Folklore   While commonly thought of as the burial place for the kings of Tara, New Grange and Tara Hill are actually much older, dating to about 3000 B.C. New Grange was uncovered in 1699 by a landowner. It was not until 1962, however, that astronomical alignments similar to those at Knowth and Dowth were discovered by reconstructing the site, which led to the idea that the site may have honored Dagda, the sun god. According to local lore, this is the home of the Tuatha de Danainn, the supernatural people birthed by the goddess Danu.

Tara Hill is the legendary seat of Irish kings, complete with a kingly fortress. In the center of the hill the Stone of Destiny rests, where all the Kings of Tara were inaugurated. This stone is also said to grant fertility and to roar three times when a future king of Ireland stands upon it.

About This Site   As you approach New Grange, you'll be dazzled by the white quartz walls that were used to rebuild the exterior. This wall is surrounded by ninety-seven large stones lying down, and twelve standing stones that remain from earlier structures. Inside, New Grange is much like other burial chambers of the region, with long tunnels and high interior domes. The difference in the New Grange corbeled vault is its size and the way the slabs were overlapped to create one stone in the center. The predominant patterns throughout New Grange are spirals (representing life's cycles and the sun), lozenges (for the feminine aspect), and arches (the meeting place between worlds).

Across the valley from New Grange is Tara Hill, a huge earth-work that looks strikingly like a Celtic torc in design. While not nearly as visually impressive as New Grange, Tara Hill has several megaliths and passages to explore, and people in the New age Community feel there are powerful ley lines here.

Activities   Because much of New Grange is underground, the womb of the earth wraps round you with force here, but the underlying sun energy is undeniable. In this manner, New Grange unites Father Sun with Mother Earth in a loving embrace that will stir the soul's memories and talents to awakening. Bring a notebook with you in case you get flashes of past lives or future paths!

Both Tara and New Grange have strong fertile aspects, so if you need increased productivity in any area of your life, this is an excellent location to try this spell: Take a pale green piece of rope (the color of early sprouts) and dust this with soil from both Tara's Hill and New Grange. Tie the rope with thirteen knots (the number of a complete lunar cycle), focusing on your goal. If you wish, add a verbal component like *Dagda, Danu bring to me your abundant fertility*. Repeat this each time you tie a knot. Release one knot when you need to likewise release the associated energy to your home or life. (Note: Fertility here doesn't have to mean just the physical—it can be figurative, like blossoming spiritual awareness or talents, a prolific imagination, a thriving garden, etc.)

Side Trips   Take a trip to Cork, specifically the tiny village of Blarney to see the Blarney Stone and kiss it if you wish (this isn't easy, by the way, as the stone is located on a precipice). No one is sure how the tradition of kissing the stone came about, but as local poems tell us, *"a stone there, that whoever kisses; oh he never misses to grow eloquent . . ."*

THUNDER BAY, ONTARIO, CANADA
Elements: Water, earth
Themes: Spirituality, crystal awareness

Located at the northernmost point of Lake Superior, Ontario, Canada, the Bay and all its facilities are easily accessible by major highways in Ontario. Hotels, motels, and an airport are all available in Thunder Bay proper.

To enjoy the over 150 parks throughout this region and its rock climbing, the best time to travel is around May, just after the spring thaw. Otherwise, you'll hit a lot of snow or heavy rains. For snow lovers, however, winter offers fantastic skiing and snowmobile trails.

Specific information can be obtained through the visitor's information center at 800-667-8386 or on-line at: www.tourism. thunder-bay.on.ca

History and Folklore   Best known today as the home of the Terry Fox memorial, the brave young man who ran across Ontario with an artificial leg, Thunder Bay has a rich history as a central site of the fur trade. It is also the home to the Ojibwa tribe, whose arts and crafts beautify many of the area's homes, shops, and galleries.

About This Site   This region has one of the largest forest preserves on the North American continent, making for beautiful scenery. Old Fort William is located here, complete with forty-two historic buildings from the 1800s, a wharf, primitive apothecary, and Ojibwa arts and crafts. The fort is only open from May through October, 10 A.M. to 5 P.M.

If you want to get a good feel for regional history and tradition, go to the Thunder Bay History Museum, founded in 1908. Here you'll get to see 10,000-year-old native tools, beadwork, embroidery, fur trade relics, and other historical archives. The museum is open from 11–5 daily during the summer, and 1–5 Tuesday through Thursday in the winter.

Beyond these kinds of sites, Thunder Bay is home to nine amethyst mines, which create a resonating energy that cannot be missed. You can walk into the mines themselves and select whatever stone calls to you. In esoteric traditions, the amethyst represents matters of spirituality, magic, and self-control.

Activities   Definitely go rock hunting! When you find an amethyst you want to keep, leave another stone or offering for the land in its place (this shows respect and reciprocity to the gnomish spirits who tend the crystals). Meditate with your chosen stone so it harmonizes with your energy. You'll then be able to use the crystal in numerous magical settings as a key-stone for focusing energy, especially spells and rituals designed to deepen spiritual awareness, manifest inner peace, inspire intelligent thought, improve business success, and protect from negativity.

Side Trip   Out in the bay itself is a huge stone monolith called the Sleeping Giant, which is open from May to October. The Marie Louise campground is very closeby for people who wish to camp while visiting the site. This area will be of partic-ular interest to flower lovers, as it hosts a number of wild orchid species, including some rare varieties. There is also a visitor's center at the park should you need directions elsewhere or more information.

THUNDERHEAD FALLS, SOUTH DAKOTA
Elements: Water, earth
Themes: Cleansing, healing, prosperity, peace, dreams

Thunderhead Falls is but ten miles away from Rapid City, South Dakota, along Highway 44 West. Rapid City offers numerous options for accommodations, but I suggest considering a stay at the Four Winds Ranch (www.fourwindsranch.com or 605-673-5176). The facilities here are designed for spiritual seekers who want to bridge the gap between Native American traditions and their own paths. The ranch advocates multicultural exchange and earth-awareness, and the people here will happily provide you with tons of local history and lore to fill your free hours.

For more information, contact the site directly at 605-343-0081, Rapid City Visitors Bureau at 800-487-3233, or refer to the on-line tourism information available at: www.state.sd.us/state/executive/tourism or www.pahasapa.com.

History and Folklore The name among the Lakotah Sioux indians for this region is Paha Sapa, and it's considered an abode for the gods to this tribe and to the Cheyenne. In looking at the area, it's easy to see why such an association came about. Here the trees are god's temples, the lakes are his/her mirror, the caves house divine treasures, the wildlife is abundant, and the stars shine brightly, guiding our way back home.

Native Americans often came to this area seeking visions and to purify themselves. This was also where various warring tribes could meet in peace to discuss their differences.

About This Site   In sharp contrast to the Black Hills that surround it, Thunderhead Falls is a truly unique waterfall located 600 feet inside a mountain! Here 8 cubic feet of water falls over 30 feet through an old gold mine. The combination of water and earth, with the history of the gold rush, combine here for profuse energies that can be applied to many of life's needs.

All around the site great buffalo graze lazily, prairie dogs sing, coyotes howl, and for a moment you're transported to America's Old West. Perhaps this is why some of the Sioux call the Black Hills "dream catchers."

Activities   There's a lot of potential energy to tap into here. Sprinkle an herb that represents a specific goal into the water, then follow up with other significant actions to help manifest that goal. Use dried marigold petals for psychic dreams (put a few of these under your pillow at night), lavender or violet to inspire peace with yourself or another (make the leftovers into a sachet), orange rind or almonds for prosperity (carry some afterward in your wallet as a charm to draw money to you), marjoram and thyme for health (drink a tea of this afterward), and sage for purification (put some in your bath).

Side Trips   Black Hills Caverns are located on Highway 44 from I-90, just four miles west of Rapid City. These caves have a very similar energy to Thunderhead except they're more strongly aligned to earth than water. Within, you'll find popcorn helictites, stalagmites, logomites, frost crystal, flowstone, spar, boxwork, cave flowers, and much more to please any cave lover. These caverns were discovered in the 1880s by people seeking gold, and, in a way, they found it—nature's treasures beautifully preserved through rain water seeping through various minerals and depositing the crystals. The phone number for the park is 800-837-9558.

TIAHUANACO, BOLIVIA
Elements: Fire, water:
Themes: God, sun/moon magic, miracles, beginning, balance

The Tiahuanaco ruins are located on the western border of Bolivia near Sopocaci (one hour away). For a large variety of accommodations and amenities you'll want to stay in La Paz, the capital city. However, this is at least four hours away from the site. So, it might be worth your while to check into accommodations in Sopocaci for a day or so, where you can easily get a tour and local guides.

Be aware that the air here is thin. You'll want to spend your first day taking it slow and eating simple foods to acclimate to the environment. This will make your stay far more pleasant and comfortable. For more information, contact the Bolivian Embassy at 202-483-4410.

History and Folklore Legends tell us that Tiahuanaco was created in one night by bearded giants who descended from the clouds. It was to this wondrous place that the Incan god Viracocha, the creator of the sun, moon, and stars, traveled from his home in the lake to help humankind. It's interesting to note that he is sometimes depicted with fish scales—this alludes to his watery abode and is a symbol often connected with savior figures!

The truth is a little less romantic. Historians believe the city was created by Incan predecessors about 2,000 years ago. It is speculated in some native studies that the city may have been inhabited long before that, but these theories have not been verified.

About This Site This city, one of the oldest in the world, lies at 12,500 feet above sea level and is made of stones, some of which weigh over 150 tons. The Kalasasaya courtyard (a name meaning "place of standing stones"), on the site measures the sun's movement and is akin to an over-sized clock. On the first day of spring the sun rises here through the center archway, which has an image of a deity holding two staves (as if to support the sky). The other cornerstones mark the remaining seasons. It's likely that this temple honored an early version of Viracocha. Other structures have obvious religious significance, including a huge idol that likely also represented Viracocha or a guardian spirit for the area.

Activities   Viracocha's fire brings us the sun, symbolizing strength, hope, courage, and the spark of magic. His water brings the moon, insight, spirituality, and psychism. Together, these represent a powerful balance that can be re-established in your soul with a little creative effort while here.

So, appeal to Viracocha as an aspect of the masculine force of the universe for improved symmetry in your life, to bless the beginning of any project or relationship, or if you need a figurative miracle. Burnt offerings are a very acceptable means of so doing (perhaps incense, especially a blend of fire-water herbs like frankincense and myrrh). To improve the effect of your offering, make your gift of frankincense by the rising sun, sprinkling some of it clockwise and burning the rest. Make your gift of myrrh at moonrise, sprinkling it counterclockwise and burning the rest, then putting it out with water. Adding these ritualistic elements will give more form and meaning to your time here and will help you better connect with this vibrant's god's energy.

Side Trips   Bolivia offers much to fill a traveler's itinerary. You can follow Incan trails, go on jungle tours, bird watch, explore native craft work, climb mountains, go sailing, or walk through tropical valleys. Specifically, more in keeping with Tiahuanaco's theme, just thirteen miles away, lies Lake Titicaca, also called the Sun Island, where Viracocha sent his son and daughter to teach humans not only how to survive, but various creative arts like weaving as well.

Uluru (Ayers Rock), Australia
Elements: Earth, air
Themes: Dreams, knowledge/learning, time, the Goddess

Uluru is part of Kata Tjuta National Park, located about four hours southwest of Alice Springs. You can find camping and resort facilities right at the park entrance (eighteen kilometers from Uluru), along with restaurants and gas stations. It is well worth staying here for convenience and cultural appeal since the Aboriginal people put on traditional dance and music programs during park hours and offer souvenirs. The park is wheelchair-accessible

If you travel during August, you can go to Queensland for the Outback Festival, which celebrates the pioneer traditions. For information on this particular event or more information about Uluru or travel in general, contact the Central Australia Tourist Industry Association at 011-618-8-952-5199, the Department of the Environment at 011-618-6-274-1111, or the park directly at 011-618-8-956-3138.

History and Folklore   Uluru is the most famous landmark of the land "down under." It is completely natural, having been formed by sediments from an ancient sea. These sediments were pushed upward over thousands of years, which is easy to see from the layering in the rock.

Local legends tell us that two children created the monolith while playing in the rain during dreamtime. Other stories say the ancestors formed the rock at the beginning of creation, leaving it there to remind the Aboriginal people of their connection to, and stewardship of, the land. The Aborigines regard the land's protection as a sacred duty, which is why they still request that people not climb Uluru. In recent years this area has been declared a biosphere reserve due to its rich flora and fauna.

About This Site   Uluru is the world's largest monolith. It makes for a very impressive site, rising 348 meters above the surrounding desert. Yet despite its size, it's thought that about two-thirds of Ayers (Uluru) still lies hidden beneath the ground! Travelers are allowed to walk the 1.6 kilometers around the rock if accompanied by a native guide, who can tell them about the site and its importance in dreamtime legends.

This is not the only site to enjoy in the park, however. Many Aboriginal sacred places dot the countryside, including dreaming paths and rock art caves. There are also mystical rock formations like the Kata Tjuta, thirty-six dome-shaped rocks that tower up to 1,700 feet tall and are located in the Valley of the Winds. The name means "many heads," which gives the region an air of intelligence all its own. From a distance Kata Tjuta looks like a woman's body. Natives consider it a sacred place for women or a place to connect with goddess energies.

Activities   Go to Kata Tjuta at sunset (about a thirty-minute drive) and listen as the light touches on the stones. You can almost audibly hear the music of the ages as the stone's colors turn from rust to pink and near-purple. Learn that song, and sing a magical song of your own to harmonize with the timeless energy. Visualize the colors in the stones and the sunlight saturating your forehead for clear thought that doesn't discount the intuitive nature.

Sleep beneath Uluru one night, asking the ancestors for a spiritual dream. Then watch the sunrise here so the light can ignite fresh energy to pursue that vision. Or, walk one of the ancient trails and pathways that the Aborigines used for personal vision quests and other rituals. As you go, open yourself to nature's omens and signs to see what messages the earth wishes to convey.

Finally, venture to the southern side of Uluru to see the Laughing Cave, which looks distinctly like a mouth open in uproarious laughter. It is a good place to renew your sense of joy in life.

Side Trips   Most travelers recommend stopping to see Kings Canyon, which is about three hundred kilometers away

from the main entrance of the park. Here you'll find two spectacular formations known as the Lost City and Garden of Eden.
If possible, take the walk around the rim of the canyon to get a
bird's eye view. Tours are available through the park facilities.

VALLEY OF THE MONUMENTS, UTAH
Element: Fire
Theme: Truthfulness

Located on the Utah-Arizona border, the monuments are nearest to the town of Goulding, which was a trading post in the
early 1900s and has definite Old World charm. The main road
here is U.S. 163, which passes near the monuments but doesn't
venture much among them. Monument Park is a Navaho reservation and costs approximately $5 to get in. There is a historical
museum here, with relics and a gift shop that's open from 8–6
nearly year-round.

Travel to the valley during late spring. It's very quiet during
this season, allowing for thoughtful meditation. Camper-trailers
are perhaps the best mode of transportation, providing you with
the freedom to stop wherever you wish to enjoy the scenery. For
more information, contact the Arizona Tourism department at
800-842-8257.

History and Folklore Calling themselves *dineh* (the
people), the Navaho people inhabited vast expanses of this
region for hundreds of years until westward settlers pushed
them back to what now consists of 25,000 miles of reservation.
Around the region the history, the culture, ritual, and lore of the
Navahos have not been lost, though. The valley has no running
water or electricity, which creates a rather timeless and
untouched feeling. In addition, most natives still hold regular
rituals here, and traditional weaving is still a major source of
income and trade.

Weary travelers can sit and talk to members of the tribe, who will happily share lore and superstitions. If, for example, you happen to have a coyote cross your path during your journey, it represents bad luck. Don't look at the full moon while sightseeing or your future children will be born needing glasses. And always keep your shoes tied while walking. This keeps away any evil influences.

About This Site   Not in an actual valley, monuments like Castle Rock make an impressive display against the flatlands and crumbling stones around them, especially at sunrise and sunset. The reddish sandstone mingles with the light in the sky, creating a marvelous display of colors for camera-happy travelers.

The best scenic tour is along a 17-mile dirt road that shows off cliffs, mesas, and rock spires, including the famous Totem Pole monument that rises 300 feet high seemingly out of nowhere. Unfortunately, unless you have a four-wheel-drive vehicle, the road is difficult to traverse. Consider going with a native guide instead, who will likely also be able to access the Eye of the Sun monument, which can only be viewed with a licensed guide. Fees run approximately $15 for three hours.

Activities   Some people go to the desert to "find" themselves, but those who have done so don't recommend it to others. This region's spiritual teachers are brutally honest and truthful with those who visit. If you go in fear, you will find fear; if you go in hope and worshipfulness, you will find enlightenment.

Gather a little sand during your journeys and put it in a medicine bundle to remind yourself to stay true to your ideals and taboos. Sprinkle just a pinch any time you feel a situation could use some candidness.

Side Trips   The Valley of the Gods is thirty miles north on Route 163. These ancient red sandstone pillars rise up to greet the Great Spirit, giving the valley its name. The valley is near the town of Mexican Hat. You can find guest information here and free camping along with a great view of the San Juan River.

VIRGINIA BEACH, VIRGINIA
Elements: Water, air
Themes: Meditation, prophesy, manifestation

Nestled in the heart of the mid-Atlantic Coast, the tourist season at the beach runs May through September. A variety of lodging is plentiful throughout the area, including bed-and-breakfast facilities that are often quaint and wonderfully private.

Peak times for travel occur during school recesses. This sometimes causes traffic jams and overcrowded conditions, so time your trip bearing this in mind. Further travel information is available on-line at: travelfile.com/get?vabch.

History and Folklore   In 1607 settlers landed at Cape Henry in northern Virginia Beach. By the late 1600s many had homes in Jamestown, part of the same county in which Virginia Beach remains. It's only been considered a resort area for about a hundred years, and it also became the home to the Association for Research and Enlightenment (ARE)—the organization founded by visionary Edgar Cayce, also known as the sleeping prophet.

About This Site   Virginia Beach has an interesting mix of Old World and New World sights, sounds, and feelings. During tourist season, there are water sports, fishing, golf, tennis, yachting, sightseeing boats, historic homes, the Marine Science Museum, an amusement park, and the Seashore State Park to keep a visitor busy. In off-season the beach becomes quiet, and for a spiritual seeker, this might be the best time to go. Then, you can walk alone and work with the shoreline's energy.

Activities   If you'd like to visit the ARE, they have a fantastic library of materials on psychism and many other metaphysical topics. They're located at 67th and Atlantic Avenues.

I personally just like taking in the beach at sunrise or sunset. During sunrise meditations, I draw in the sand a symbol of an attribute that I'd like to develop in my life, then let the sun and

water kiss it into manifestation. At sunset, I allow the same water and darkness to take away things I don't need.

Also, collect a small piece of driftwood for yourself. Keep this on your altar to honor the water element, use it as a wand, or grind it up as a base for water/lunar incense.

WHITEFACE MOUNTAIN, NEW YORK
Elements: Air, earth
Themes: Rejuvenation, cycles, ecology

Whiteface Mountain is located in the heart of the Adirondack Mountains, adjacent to Lake Placid, New York (the site of the Olympic Winter Games in 1980). If you're traveling here by car, I suggest going before the winter sets in—the curving roads through the mountains and hills are quite dangerous when snow covered.

Lodging isn't a problem for visitors. Lake Placid has numerous facilities in the Olympic village. Or, for a quieter location, try Saranac Lake nearby. For on-line tourist information, refer to www.adirondaks.com.

History and Folklore   Whiteface Mountain's impressive white slopes have sat quietly for ages, watching the development of this region. During the 1800s miners and farmers began settling here. Local people claim that on a quiet day you can sit on the mountain and still hear the miners tapping out veins.

Come the late nineteenth century, the Adirondacks were a favored vacation spot for the affluent and have remained a tourist site to this day. More recently, an air-testing observatory was established on the mountain, specifically for monitoring air purity and temperature for ecological reasons.

About This Site   As part of the Adirondack State Park, you can enjoy quiet walks along foot trails, camping, fishing, and climbing. If you travel in the winter and like snow-related activities, this region is a mecca! Whiteface Mountain and the neighboring resorts offer some of the best downhill skiing, cross-country skiing, ice skating, tobogganing, dog sled rides, and snowboarding in North America.

For naturalists, there are over 50 species of animals, 220 different types of birds, and 30 species of reptiles for which to watch. In addition, you can take a side trip for Saranac Lake's annual ice-carving exhibition, which dots the town with spectacular frozen art.

Activities   Early autumn is my favorite time of the year to visit. It is one of the most spectacular places to observe the changing leaves, which present a bouquet of colors. This is an excellent opportunity to sit on a peak and meditate about life's cycles and the ever-changing Wheel of Time. If you're lucky, you'll catch a falling oak leaf before it reaches the earth and be assured of a sniffle-free winter!

Take a leisurely walk up the side of Whiteface Mountain (there are stairs and viewing ledges along the way). Stand in the crisp, cool air and let it fill you. As you breath, release any anxiety and feel the winds refreshing your spirit. Sense the ancient earth beneath your feet and the stability it offers. Look out upon the earth, your home.

WIND CAVE, SOUTH DAKOTA
Element: Air
Themes: Rejuvenation, creativity, communication

Wind Cave is located off RR 1 in Hot Springs, South Dakota, central to the Black Hills in Sioux country. For the scenic route, try Wildlife Loop Road or Needles Highway (SD 87) to access the park. The towns of Custer and Hot Springs offer camping and lodging, as does the park itself.

Cave tours are available year-round, including a candlelight tour that is romantic, timeless, and a little unearthly. Do not attempt the longer tours unless you're physically fit, as many require bending and climbing numerous stairs (100–400+), and some age restrictions may apply. The visitors center will arrange tours for those with special needs on request.

If you can travel late in July, you'll be treated to the Gold Discovery Days, a five-day festival that includes a street fair, balloon races, sports, and music. For more information, call the park at 605-745-4600, the South Dakota Tourism bureau at 800-952-3625, or review the site on-line at nps.gov/wica.

History and Folklore   Formed over 300 million years ago, Wind Cave became America's seventh National Park in 1903. It was originally discovered in 1881, thanks to a loud whistle sound that led two brothers, Jesse and Tom Bringham, to a hole in the ground connected to Wind Cave. The air blowing out of the hole was strong enough to knock Jesse's hat off, and thus the cave earned its name. You'll notice this breeze at the cave's entrance.

About This Site Wind Cave Park offers a variety of wildlife, grasslands, low rolling hills dotted with pines, ravines, and preserved prairie land. Besides this, the caves themselves seem like a fantasy landscape dotted with boxwork, popcorn, honeycomb calcite, and frostwork formations. Some of these formations are so delicate or intricate that they look like animals and plants, resulting in some chambers with names like Garden of Eden.

Activities Magical tradition says that witches can whistle up the wind. This seems to me like a perfect place to learn! Listen to the sound the cave makes and try to mimic it. The next time you need more energy, to communicate effectively or to get inspired, repeat this whistle three times and let the magic of this sacred site manifest your will!

Side Trips Other places of interest within an hour's drive include Mt. Rushmore and Jewel Cave, which is filled with calcite formations.

WYANDOTTE CAVES, INDIANA
Element: Double earth
Themes: Foundations, grounding, worship

The Wyandotte cave system is located on State Road 62 in Crawford County, Indiana. Fees for visiting this site depend on the kind of tour you undertake. They range from under $2 to $12, depending on length and theme, and most tours take place at regular intervals daily. Some tours, however, are seasonal or require reservations so inquire ahead. The park phone number is 812-738-2782.

Wyandotte has camping available along with other activities for travelers, including horse trails, picnic areas, fishing, and canoeing. Alternatively, consider staying in Leavenworth, which has some bed-and-breakfast facilities. For more information about lodging, call 800-739-4263 or 888-739-2120. You can also refer to www.cccn.net for details about Crawford County.

History and Folklore   There are strong indications that prehistoric people worshiped here, such as the discovery of ashes, twisted wood pieces, and fragments chipped from the formations. The boundary of the Wyandotte system is also dotted with relic Indian mounds. More than likely, the natives recognized the voice of the Mother in the land and were honoring it in their own way.

About This Site   Wyandotte Caves are nestled neatly in the heart of three thousand acres of timberland bordering on the Ohio River, which makes for amazing scenery, especially come the fall. The park itself has different tours that you can take. The Little Wyandotte tour is short and easy, showing smaller caves and a view of flowstone and dripstone formations like Cleopatra's Palace. There's a historical tour to parts of the caves not open since lantern tours were available. The Monument Mountain tour goes deeper into the caves so you can see rare formations, flint quarries, and gypsum sections.

One of the most challenging tours is to the Pillar of the Constitution. It takes half a day up through an old cave and several tight fits, to a huge limestone formation. There's also a full-day tour to sites aptly named Worm Alley and Milroy's Temple.

Activities   One thing you should not miss is spending time at Monument Mountain, an underground mass created by fallen rock, capped with stalagmites, that reaches 185 feet in height. The combination of a cave (womb) with the rocky butte creates double earth energies here. It is nearly impossible to stand at the base of this monument and not feel "connected." If you're prone to flights of fancy, gather a little soil or a tiny rock from this place and put it in your shoe to help you keep one foot on the ground.

Side Trip Angel Mounds, located in southwestern Indiana, are an important Native American site of a well-preserved ceremonial and social center. Several mounds here were constructed strictly for ritual use. Angel Mounts State Historic Site offers regular activities and lectures, including ones on Indian culture, archaeoastrology, and healing goddesses! Information about park hours, rates, and so forth can be obtained by calling 812-853-3956. The closest town to Angel Mounds is Evansville, which is quite used to tourists. For lodging and other information, call 800-433-3025, or e-mail tourism@evansvillecvb.org.

A second site worth going to is New Harmony, a town just northwest of Angel Mounds, founded by a utopian religious community. By far the most interesting feature here (other than the history of the community) is a labyrinth setting on the south end of the town. This carefully maintained grouping of bushes is a reconstruction of an earlier pattern that was likely designed to mirror the universe's ebb and flow for all walking it. New Harmony offers lodging and camping if you find you want to make this more than a day trip.

ZIMBABWE, AFRICA
Element: Earth
Themes: Herbalism, intercession, prosperity, weather, history

The ruins of Great Zimbabwe are located in Zimbabwe, Southeast Africa. For comfort and convenience there is a hotel on the perimeter of the site, or you can stay in Masuingo, the provincial capital, which has hotels, bed-and-breakfast accommodations, and other tourist amenities. Masuingo is just seventeen miles from the site and you can arrange for tours from here easily.

In terms of travel time, you can catch an interesting festival between June and October. At this time of the year the Makonde people celebrate a rite of passage for their young adults by performing masked dances through many villages. For more information, call the Zimbabwe Tourist Office at 800-621-2381 or refer to www.zimweb.com or www.zimbabwe.net/tourism.

History and Folklore   There is no question that the Great Zimbabwe ruins represent the greatest histo-religious remains in southern Africa. In fact, the construction here was so impressive that the people who rediscovered the site attributed it to the Greeks until more research was done. We now know that this site was inhabited as early as A.D., 300 with the population reaching its height around the year 1400, at which time more than 40,000 people lived here.

During its full glory days, the Great Zimbabwe was a religious and cultural center where the chief interceded with the ancestors and land spirits on behalf of the people. The word *Zimbabwe* can translate into "honored houses," implying that these people regarded not just temples, but also their homes and village, as sacred.

About This Site   Zimbabwe's abundant plant life is likely to strike you almost immediately, numbering over 5,000 flowering species, many of which have medicinal value. This makes Zimbabwe a mecca for herbalists and homeopaths.

The ruins of Zimbabwe were created from regular, granite stones placed one atop the other without the aid of masonry. The city has several areas, one of which seems to enjoy its enigmatic nature. Called the Conical Tower, this 33-foot-high tower seems to have no entrance, despite having a hallway leading up to it. To this day, no one has gotten inside, leading to the hypothesis that the inside of the tower may be filled completely with stone or earth.

The Main Complex is a round enclosure where many people lived, to stay close to the central religious center. There's also a hill ruin to the north that was part of Zimbabwe's earliest history. This sanctuary houses monoliths, some depicting birds that, in this culture, are messengers from spirit. Offerings were left in this edifice to ensure prosperity to a family or improved weather for the whole settlement.

Activities   It is said that if you stand very, very quietly at the walls here, you can hear the memories of the past whisper to you—that you will hear bits of history. Exactly what message the stones bear for you is purely personal.

During any private moments, the Great Zimbabwe ruins are the perfect place to accept your role as the priest or priestess of your life, and intercede on your own behalf with the divine, along with prayers for anyone you know who has need. Whisper your prayer for prosperity, or perhaps for assistance in learning the herbal arts, in the Main Complex. If possible, take something with you to leave an offering to the spirits and the gods in thankfulness for their aid.

Side Trips   In Bulawayo you can see the Matopos with its unique paintings dating back to 1000 B.C. Rather than being realistic depictions, however, these seem to have been created to evoke emotional reactions or to create energy through colors and shapes.

PARTING THOUGHTS

In reading this book and others like it, you'll notice that certain parts of the world seem to have more recognized sacred sites than others. The densest areas with well-known sites include:

- Around the perimeter of Africa
- Along the Eastern Desert of the Red Sea
- Israel, Jordan, Lebanon
- Iraq, Iran
- Southern Greece

- Eastern Europe
- The United Kingdom (often near water)
- Between the Black Sea and the Caspian Sea
- The perimeter of the United States
- Guatemala
- Along the Andes
- The perimeter of Australia
- Southern Japan
- Nepal

In reviewing this list, some things become quite apparent. First, that the entire Middle East is an important power center, which explains the constant atmosphere of upheaval—too many individuals interpreting that power differently. Second, the two most popular areas for erecting a sacred site were near a lake or ocean, or high on a mountain. Why? From a Wiccan and shamanic viewpoint the ocean is feminine and the mountain/sky masculine. Also, in many religious traditions, mountains are considered god's abode, likely because they reach (from our perspective) to the heavens. This is how we come by the humorous modern image of the guru sitting on a mountain dispensing life's secrets—from here, they can be closer to god!

So even in our whimsical moments, modern humankind is at least somewhat innately aware of the sacred, as our ancestors were. Now all we need to do is take that awareness out of moth balls and make it part of our daily life. Honoring the world's sacred sites, or making our own, is but one part of that picture, which includes changing the way we think and live everyday.

The entire earth is a sacred site if we allow it to be. That means your living room, a parking lot, the supermarket, and the old tree in the neighbor's yard have just as much magical potential as the sites described in this book. Magic, by definition, works out of space and out of time—we need not be limited by our location if our imagination is keen and our will is sure.

So, open yourself up to the potentials, sacredness, and specialness of all things, including yourself.

APPENDIXES

REGIONAL APPENDIX

Africa: Zimbabwe
Australia: Uluru (Ayers Rock)
Bermuda: Natural Arches
Bolivia: Tiahuanaco
Bulgaria: Stone Forest
Cambodia: Angkor Wat
Canada: Manitoulin Island; Perce Rock; Thunder Bay
Capri: Blue Grotto
China: Hengshan
Cypress: Rock of Aphrodite
Easter Island
Egypt: Giza Pyramid
England: Bath; Glastonbury
France: Saintes Maries de la Mer
Germany: Externstein
Greece: Knossos Palace
Greenland: Narsaq
Haiti: Saut D'Eau

Honduras: Copan
India: Ellora Caves; Ganges River
Ireland: Tara Hill and New Grange
Italy: Assisi
Japan: Fujiama
Jordan: Petra
Kashmir: Amarnath
Labrador: L'Anse Amour
Mexico: Monte Alban
Myanmar: Shwe Dagon
Nepal: Kathmandu Valley
Peru: Machu Picchu
Saudi Arabia: Mecca
Scotland: Callanish
Sicily: Ear of Dionysius
Sri Lanka: Kataragama
Tibet: Everest
Turkey: Ephesus

USA

Alaska: Denali (Mt. McKinley)

Arizona: Petrified Forest; Sunset Crater

California: Redwoods State Park; Shasta

Connecticut: Sleeping Giant

Florida: Everglades

Georgia: Dragon Hills; Keith Bridge Park; Tallulah Gorge

Hawaii: Haleakala National Park

Indiana: Wyandotte Caves

Kentucky: Mammoth Cave

Louisana: Algiers Landing

Massachusettts: Salem

Maine: Katahdin

New Mexico: Chaco Canyon; Petroglyph National Monument; Rio Grande Gorge

New York: Brushwood; Niagara Falls; Whiteface Mountain

Ohio: Serpent Mound

South Dakota: Thunderhead Falls; Wind Cave

Tennessee: Lookout Mountain

Texas: Enchanted Rock

Utah: Summum Pyramid; Valley of the Monuments

Virginia: Virginia Beach

Wisconsin: Aztlan; Circle Sanctuary

Wyoming: Bighorn Medicine Wheel; Devil's Tower

ELEMENTAL APPENDIX

Earth
Angkor Wat
Assisi
Bighorn Medicine Wheel
Brushwood
Callanish
Chaco Canyon
Copan
Devil's Tower
Dragon Hills
Ear of Dionysius
Easter Island
Ellora Caves
Enchanted Rock
Everglades
Externstein
Glastonbury
Hengshan
Katahdin
Keith Bridge Park
Knossos Palace
L'Anse Amour
Lookout Mountain
Mammoth Cave
Manitoulin
Mecca

Natural Arches
Perce Rock
Petra
Redwoods State Park
Rock of Aphrodite
Serpent Mound
Sleeping Giant
Stone Forest
Summum Pyramid
Sunset Crater
Tallulah Gorge
Tara Hill
Thunder Bay
Thunderhead Falls
Uluru
Whiteface Mountain
Wyandotte Caves
Zimbabwe

Air
Denali
Devil's Tower
Ear of Dionysius
Enchanted Rock
Hengshan
Katahdin

Lookout Mountain
Narsaq
Niagara Falls
Perce Rock
Shasta
Summum Pyramid
Uluru
Virginia Beach
Whiteface Mountain
Wind Cave

Fire
Algiers Landing
Aztalan
Blue Grotto
Chaco Canyon
Copan
Easter Island
Giza
Haleakala
Machu Picchu
Narsaq
Petrified Forest
Petra
Rio Grande Gorge
Saintes Maries de la Mer

Serpent Mound
Shasta
Shwe Dagon
Sunset Crater
Tara Hill
Tiahuanacu
Valley of the Monuments

Water
Algiers Landing
Amarnath
Bath
Blue Grotto
Brushwood
Denali
Dragon Hills
Ephesus
Everglades
Externstein
Ganges River
Katahdin
Kataragama
Keith Bridge Park
Knossos Palace
L'Anse Amour

TOPICAL APPENDIX

There are moments in everyone's life when they have a specific need or goal. When this happens, look up the subject in this appendix (or a synonym for it). Then turn to the given sacred site's activities and see if you can't apply or adapt them to help you meet whatever circumstances are facing you.

Ancestors, the: Manitoulin Island
Ancestry (Heritage):   Callanish; Sunset Crater
Anger (Ending):   Denali
Astral work: Copan; Fujiama
Attraction: Petroglyph National Monument
Balance: Haleakala; Tiahuanacu
Bardic Energy (the arts:)   Katahdin
Balance: Tiahuanacu
Banishing: Kathmandu; Sleeping Giant (greed)
Beauty: Mammoth Cave
Beginnings: Everglades
Blessing: Mecca
Chakras: Externstein
Change: Serpent Mound
Color Magic: Blue Grotto
Commitment (Devotion):   Callanish; Lookout Mountain
Communication: Ear of Dionysius; Enchanted Rock; Niagara Falls; Petra; Wind Cave

Communion: Mecca

Compromise: Haleakala

Connection: Redwoods State Park

Courage: Kathmandu; Niagara Falls

Creativity: Ellora Caves; Mammoth Cave; Manitoulin; Wind Cave

Crystals (Stones): Dragon Hills; Easter Island; Tallulah Gorge

Cycles: Amarnath; Bighorn Medicine Wheel; Tara Hill; Whiteface Mountain

Dance: Everest; Stone Forest

Death: Aztalan; L'Anse Amour

Dragons: Dragon Hills; Externstein

Dreams: Manitoulin Island; Thunderhead Falls; Uluru

Earth Magic: Glastonbury; Crete

Ecology: Easter Island; Everglades; Gaspe; Redwoods State Park; Whiteface Mountain

Emotions: Bath; Petroglyph National Monument; Salem

Empathy: Bath

Energy: Denali; Niagara Falls; Rio Grande Gorge; Fujiama

Enlightenment: Kathmandu

Fairies: Glastonbury: Redwoods State Park; Stone Forest; Tara Hill

Fertility: Amarnath; Angkor Wat; Ellora Caves; Crete; Tara Hill

Friendship: Kathmandu

God: Amarnath; Angkor Wat; Copan; Tiahuanacu

Goddess: Ephesus; Externstein; Glastonbury; Uluru

Growth: Redwoods State Park

Guidance (Counsel): Enchanted Rock; Sleeping Giant

Harmony (Accord): Bighorn Medicine Wheel; Easter Island; Summum Pyramid

Healing (Health): Bath; Bighorn Medicine Wheel; Brushwood; Rio Grand Gorge; Saut D'Eau; Shasta; Shwe Dagon; Thunderhead Falls

Herbalism: Hengshan; Zimbabwe

History: Zimbabwe

Hospitality: Petra; Saintes Maries de la Mer

Initiation: Externstein

Intercession: Zimbabwe

Invisibility: Katahdin

Joy: Shwe Dagon; Narsaq

Knot Magic: Machu Picchu
Knowledge (Learning): Uluru
Land Spirits: Manitoulin Island
Leadership: Angkor Wat; Tara Hill
Light Magic: Blue Grotto; Narsaq
Longevity: Shasta
Love: Callanish; Rock of Aphrodite; Lookout Mountain
Luck: Everest; Natural Arches; Saut D'Eau; Narsaq
Magic: Brushwood; Ephesus; Saut D'Eau
Manifestation: Virginia Beach
Meditation: Hengshan; Gaspe; Summum Pyramid; Tallulah Gorge; Virginia Beach
Mediumship: Copan
Miracles: Glastonbury; Tiahuanaco
Moon Magic: Ellroa Caves; Ephesus; Tiahuanaco
Movement (Momentum): Petroglyph National Monument
Mysteries (the): Dragon Hills; Everglades
Negativity (Banishing): Denali
Networking: Circle Sanctuary; Petra
Occult: Circle Sanctuary
Offerings: Aztalan; Enchanted Rock, L'Anse Amour
Passion: Algiers Landing; Hengshan; Rock of Aphrodite; Saut D'Eau; Shwe Dagon
Peace: Algiers Landing; Blue Grotto; Keith Bridge Park; Thunderhead Falls
Perspective: Rio Grande Gorge
Pilgrimages: Mecca
Power Objects: Aztalan
Prayer (Supplication): Kathmandu; Shwe Dagon; L'Anse Amour
Preservation: Petrified Forest
Primal Energy: Everglades
Productivity: Perce Rock
Promises: Amarnath
Prophesy: Virginia Beach
Prosperity: Angkor Wat; Thunderhead Falls; Zimbabwe
Providence: Ganges River
Purification/Cleansing: Ganges River; Mecca; Niagara Falls; Thunderhead Falls; Fujiama
Recovering Lost Items: Kataragama

Reincarnation: Amarnath; Giza
Rejuvenation: Crete; Saintes Maries de la Mer; Salem; Whiteface
  Mountain; Wind Cave
Relationships: Lookout Mountain
Religious Studies: Summum Pyramid
Ritual: Circle Sanctuary; Monte Alban
Safety (Protection): Circle Sanctuary; Denali; Devil's Tower;
  Katahdin; Petrified Forest; Rock of Aphrodite
Shamanism: Petroglyph National Monument; Sunset Crater
Sleep: Sleeping Giant
Songs/Singing: Everest
Soul Gazing: Haleakala
Spirit Communication: Hengshan
Spirituality: Shasta
Stability (Foundations): Keith Bridge Park; Stone Forest;
  Wyandotte Caves
Star Magic: Haleakala
Success: Kataragama
Sun Magic: Haleakala; Machu Picchu; Tara Hill; Tiahuanaco;
  Narsaq
Time: Copan; Redwoods State Park; Uluru
Tolerance: Ellora Caves
Transformation: Natural Arches
Truthfulness: Valley of the Monuments
Universal Awareness: Giza; Monte Alban
Universal Brotherhood: Serpent Mound
Victory: Kataragama; Natural Arches
Visions: Devil's Tower
Vitality: Shasta
Vows: Kataragama; Lookout Mountain
Water Energizing: Tallulah Gorge; L'Anse Amour
Weather: Katahdin; Zimbabwe
Wisdom: Amarnath
Wishes: Narsaq
Witchcraft: Blue Grotto; Salem
Worship: Wyandotte Caves; Fujiama
UFOs: Devil's Tower

Natural Temple Appendix

Throughout history humankind has seemed drawn to specific types of natural settings to perform magic. More interesting still is the fact that the types of magic or ritual performed in each setting are often similar. To me, this indicates an arcetype that you can use in considering where best to create a power center if it's to have a focused purpose. Here are a few examples that I observed when writing this book:

Caves: Initiation, rites of passage, visionary experience
Cliffs: Sacrifice, vision, perspective
Flowers/Gardens: Spirits, healing, love, passion
Forests: Animal kinship, sacred space
Fruit Groves: Fertility, abundance, prosperity
Hot Springs: Healing, purification, cleansing
Mountains: Communing with spirits or the divine, clarity, visions, meditation
Ocean: Fertility, transformation, growth or diminishing
Rivers: Movement and momentum, purification, offerings
Thorny Plants: Protection
Trees: Healing, wishes, strength, devic work, safety
Volcano: Offerings, banishing
Wells: Healing, wishes, weather magic (rain)

SELECTED BIBLIOGRAPHY

Bath (no noted editor). 1 the Corridor, Bath, England: Unichrome, 1983.

Bruce-Mitford, Miranda. *Illustrated Book of Signs & Symbols*. New York, NY: DK Publishing, 1996.

Conliffe, Professor. *The Roman Baths & Museum*. Bath, England: Bath Archaeologial Trust, 1985.

Davison, Michael Worth, ed. *Everyday Life Through the Ages*. Pleasantville, NY: Reader's Digest Association Ltd., 1992.

Gordon, Stuart. *Encyclopedia of Myths and Legends*. London, England: Headline Book Publishing, 1993.

Hardin, Jesse. *Full Circle: A Song of Ecology and Earthen Spirituality*. St. Paul, MN: Llewellyn Publications, 1991.

Henderson, Helene, and Sue Ellen Thompson, eds. *Holidays, Festivals and Celebrations of the World Dictionary*. Detroit, MI: Omnigraphics, 1997.

Horan, Anne, ed. *Mystic Places*. Alexandria, VA: Time Life Books, 1987.

Ingpen, Robert, and Philip Wilkenson. *Encyclopedia of Mysterious Places*. New York, NY: 1990.

Joseph, Frank. *Sacred Sites*. St. Paul, MN: Llewellyn Publications, 1992.

Leach, Maria, ed. *Standard Dictionary of Folklore, Mythology, and Legend*. New York, NY: Harper & Row, 1984.

Opie, Iona, and Moira Tatem. *A Dictionary of Superstitions*. New York, NY: Oxford University Press, 1989.

Sargent, Denny. *Global Ritualism*. St. Paul, MN: Llewellyn Publications, 1994.

Telesco, Patricia. *Futuretelling*. Freedom, CA: Crossing Press, 1997.

Telesco, Patricia. *A Healer's Handbook*. York Beach, ME: Weiser Books, 1997.

Telesco, Patricia. *Herbal Arts*. Secaucus, NJ: Citadel Books, 1997.

Westwood, Jennifer. *Sacred Journeys*. New York, NY: Henry Holt & Company, 1997.

Wheeler, William A. *Familiar Allusions*. Detroit, MI: James R. Osgood & Company, 1882.

Wilson, Colin. *Atlas of Holy Places & Sacred Sites*. New York, NY: DK Publishing, 1996.